THE ENCYCLOPEDIA OF PSYCHOACTIVE DRUGS

IN 25 VOLUMES
Each title on a specific drug or drug-related problem

HEROIN

THE ENCYCLOPEDIA OF PSYCHOACTIVE DRUGS

HEROIN:

The Street Narcotic

FRED ZACKON, M. Ed.

1986
CHELSEA HOUSE PUBLISHERS
NEW YORK
NEW HAVEN   PHILADELPHIA

SENIOR EDITOR: William P. Hansen
PROJECT EDITOR: Jane Larkin Crain
ASSISTANT EDITOR: Paula Edelson
EDITORIAL COORDINATOR: Karyn Gullen Browne
EDITORIAL STAFF: Jeff Freiert
　　　　　　　　Susan Friedman
　　　　　　　　Perry Scott King
　　　　　　　　Kathleen McDermott
　　　　　　　　Alma Rodriguez-Sokol
CAPTIONS: Elizabeth Terhune
LAYOUT: Noreen M. Lamb
ART ASSISTANTS: Carol McDougall
　　　　　　　　Victoria Tomaselli
PICTURE RESEARCH: Elizabeth Terhune
　　　　　　　　Brian Araujo

First printing

Library of Congress Cataloging in Publication Data
Zackon, Fred.
　　　Heroin: the street narcotic.

　　　(The Encyclopedia of psychoactive drugs)
　　　Bibliography: p.
　　　Includes index.
　　　1. Heroin habit—Juvenile literature.
2. Heroin—Toxicology—Juvenile literature.
3. Drug addicts—Juvenile literature.　I. Title.
II. Series.
RC568.H4Z33　1986　　　616.86'3　　　　85-31440
ISBN 0-87754-769-6

Chelsea House Publishers

133 Christopher Street, New York, NY 10014

345 Whitney Avenue, New Haven, CT 05510

5014 West Chester Pike, Edgemont, PA 19028

THE ENCYCLOPEDIA OF PSYCHOACTIVE DRUGS

HEROIN:

The Street Narcotic

FRED ZACKON, M. Ed.

1986
CHELSEA HOUSE PUBLISHERS
NEW YORK
NEW HAVEN   PHILADELPHIA

SENIOR EDITOR: William P. Hansen
PROJECT EDITOR: Jane Larkin Crain
ASSISTANT EDITOR: Paula Edelson
EDITORIAL COORDINATOR: Karyn Gullen Browne
EDITORIAL STAFF: Jeff Freiert
                 Susan Friedman
                 Perry Scott King
                 Kathleen McDermott
                 Alma Rodriguez-Sokol
CAPTIONS: Elizabeth Terhune
LAYOUT: Noreen M. Lamb
ART ASSISTANTS: Carol McDougall
                 Victoria Tomaselli
PICTURE RESEARCH: Elizabeth Terhune
                 Brian Araujo

First printing

Library of Congress Cataloging in Publication Data
Zackon, Fred.
    Heroin: the street narcotic.

    (The Encyclopedia of psychoactive drugs)
    Bibliography: p.
    Includes index.
    1. Heroin habit—Juvenile literature.
2. Heroin—Toxicology—Juvenile literature.
3. Drug addicts—Juvenile literature. I. Title.
II. Series.
RC568.H4Z33 1986   616.86′3   85-31440
ISBN 0-87754-769-6

Chelsea House Publishers

133 Christopher Street, New York, NY 10014

345 Whitney Avenue, New Haven, CT 05510

5014 West Chester Pike, Edgemont, PA 19028

CONTENTS

First Lady Nancy Reagan was pleased to appear on the television show "Different Strokes" because she felt it offered the chance to communicate to millions of young people the dangers of drug abuse.

FOREWORD

In the Mainstream of American Life

The rapid growth of drug use and abuse is one of the most dramatic changes in the fabric of American society in the last 20 years. The United States has the highest level of psychoactive drug use of any industrialized society. It is 10 to 30 times greater than it was 20 years ago.

According to a recent Gallup poll, young people consider drugs the leading problem that they face. One of the legacies of the social upheaval of the 1960s is that psychoactive drugs have become part of the mainstream of American life. Schools, homes, and communities cannot be "drug proofed." There is a demand for drugs—and the supply is plentiful. Social norms have changed and drugs are not only available—they are everywhere.

Almost all drug use begins in the preteen and teenage years. These years are few in the total life cycle, but critical in the maturation process. During these years adolescents face the difficult tasks of discovering their identity, clarifying their sexual roles, asserting their independence, learning to cope with authority, and searching for goals that will give their lives meaning. During this intense period of growth, conflict is inevitable and the temptation to use drugs is great. Drugs are readily available, adolescents are curious and vulnerable, there is peer pressure to experiment, and there is the temptation to escape from conflicts.

No matter what their age or socioeconomic status, no group is immune to the allure and effects of psychoactive drugs. The U.S. Surgeon General's report, "Healthy People," indicates that 30% of all deaths in the United States

This woman sits alone facing a wall where she was told to sit by former narcotics addicts who run a treatment program. The addict's desire to change is essential to a successful recovery from an opiate dependency.

are premature because of alcohol and tobacco use. However, the most shocking development in this report is that mortality in the age group between 15 and 24 has increased since 1960 despite the fact that death rates for all other age groups have declined in the 20th century. Accidents, suicides, and homicides are the leading cause of death in young people 15 to 24 years of age. In many cases the deaths are directly related to drug use.

THE ENCYCLOPEDIA OF PSYCHOACTIVE DRUGS answers the questions that young people are likely to ask about drugs, as well as those they might not think to ask, but should. Topics include: what it means to be intoxicated; how drugs affect mood; why people take drugs; who takes them; when they take them; and how much they take. They will learn what happens to a drug when it enters the body. They will learn what it means to get "hooked" and how it happens. They will learn how drugs affect their driving, their schoolwork, and those around them—their peers, their family, their friends, and their employers. They will learn what the signs are that indicate that a friend or a family member may have a drug problem and to identify four stages leading from drug use to drug abuse. Myths about drugs are dispelled.

National surveys indicate that students are eager for information about drugs and that they respond to it. Students not only need information about drugs—they want information. How they get it often proves crucial. Providing young people with accurate knowledge about drugs is one of the most critical aspects.

THE ENCYCLOPEDIA OF PSYCHOACTIVE DRUGS synthesizes the wealth of new information in this field and demystifies this complex and important subject. Each volume in the series is written by an expert in the field. Handsomely illustrated, this multi-volume series is geared for teenage readers. Young people will read these books, share them, talk about them, and make more informed decisions because of them.

Miriam Cohen, Ph.D.
Contributing Editor

The babies of mothers who are addicted to opiates are often born with a narcotics dependency themselves. Clara Hale, 79, runs a foster home to care for the infants of drug addicts.

INTRODUCTION

The Gift of Wizardry
Use and Abuse

JACK H. MENDELSON, M.D.

NANCY K. MELLO, PH.D.

Alcohol and Drug Abuse Research Center
Harvard Medical School—McLean Hospital

Dorothy to the Wizard:

"I think you are a very bad man," said Dorothy.
"Oh, no, my dear; I'm really a very good man; but I'm a very bad Wizard."

—from THE WIZARD OF OZ

Man is endowed with the gift of wizardry, a talent for discovery and invention. The discovery and invention of substances that change the way we feel and behave are among man's special accomplishments, and like so many other products of our wizardry, these substances have the capacity to harm as well as to help. The substance itself is neutral, an intricate molecular structure. Yet, "too much" can be sickening, even deadly. It is man who decides how each substance is used, and it is man's beliefs and perceptions that give this neutral substance the attributes to heal or destroy.

Consider alcohol—available to all and yet regarded with intense ambivalence from biblical times to the present day. The use of alcoholic beverages dates back to our earliest ancestors. Alcohol use and misuse became associated with the worship of gods and demons. One of the most powerful Greek gods was Dionysus, lord of fruitfulness and god of wine. The Romans adopted Dionysus but changed his name to Bacchus. Festivals and holidays associated with Bacchus celebrated the harvest and the origins of life. Time has blurred the images of the Bacchanalian festival, but the theme of drunkenness as a major part of celebration has survived the pagan gods and remains a familiar part of modern society.

The term "Bacchanalian festival" conveys a more appealing image than "drunken orgy" or "pot party," but whatever the label, some of the celebrants will inevitably start up the "high" escalator to the next plateau. Once there, the de-escalation is difficult for many.

According to reliable estimates, one out of every ten Americans develops a serious alcohol-related problem sometime in his or her lifetime. In addition, automobile accidents caused by drunken drivers claim the lives of tens of thousands every year. Many of the victims are gifted young people, just starting out in adult life. Hospital emergency rooms abound with patients seeking help for alcohol-related injuries.

Who is to blame? Can we blame the many manufacturers who produce such an amazing variety of alcoholic beverages? Should we blame the educators who fail to explain the perils of intoxication, or so exaggerate the dangers of drinking that no one could possibly believe them? Are friends to blame— those peers who urge others to "drink more and faster," or the macho types who stress the importance of being able to "hold your liquor"? Casting blame, however, is hardly constructive, and pointing the finger is a fruitless way to deal with problems. Alcoholism and drug abuse have few culprits but many victims. Accountability begins with each of us, every time we choose to use or to misuse an intoxicating substance.

It is ironic that some of man's earliest medicines, derived from natural plant products, are used today to poison and to intoxicate. Relief from pain and suffering is one of society's many continuing goals. Over 3,000 years ago, the Therapeutic Papyrus of Thebes, one of our earliest written records, gave instructions for the use of opium in the treatment of pain. Opium, in the form of its major derivative, morphine, remains one of the most powerful drugs we have for pain relief. But opium, morphine, and similar compounds, such as heroin, have also been used by many to induce changes in mood and feeling. Another example of man's misuse of a natural substance is the coca leaf, which for centuries was used by the Indians of Peru to reduce fatigue and hunger. Its modern derivative, cocaine, has important medical use as a local anesthetic. Unfortunately, its increasing abuse in the 1980s has reached epidemic proportions.

The purpose of this series is to provide information about the nature and behavioral effects of alcohol and drugs, and the probable consequences of their use. The information presented here (and in other books in this series) is based on many clinical and laboratory studies and observations by people from diverse walks of life.

Over the centuries, novelists, poets, and dramatists have provided us with many insights into the beneficial and problematic aspects of alcohol and drug use. Physicians, lawyers, biologists, psychologists, and social scientists have contributed to a better understanding of the causes and consequences of using these substances. The authors in this series have attempted to gather and condense all the latest information about drug use and abuse. They have also described the sometimes wide gaps in our knowledge and have suggested some new ways to answer many difficult questions.

One such question, for example, is how do alcohol and drug problems get started? And what is the best way to treat them when they do? Not too many years ago, alcoholics and drug abusers were regarded as evil, immoral, or both. It is now recognized that these persons suffer from very complicated diseases involving complex biological, psychological, and social problems. To understand how the disease begins and progresses, it is necessary to understand the nature of the substance, the behavior and genetic makeup of the afflicted person, and the characteristics of the society or culture in which he lives.

The diagram below shows the interaction of these three factors. The arrows indicate that the substance not only affects the user personally, but the society as well. Society influences attitudes towards the substance, which in turn affect its availability. The substance's impact upon the society may support or discourage the use and abuse of that substance.

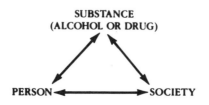

SUBSTANCE
(ALCOHOL OR DRUG)

PERSON ← → SOCIETY

Although many of the social environments we live in are very similar, some of the most subtle differences can strongly influence our thinking and behavior. Where we live, go to school and work, whom we discuss things with—all influence our opinions about drug use and misuse. Yet we also share certain commonly accepted beliefs that outweigh any differences in our attitudes. The authors in this series have tried to identify and discuss the central, most crucial issues concerning drug use and misuse.

Regrettably, man's wizardry in developing new substances in medical therapeutics has not always been paralleled by intelligent usage. Although we do know a great deal about the effects of alcohol and drugs, we have yet to learn how to impart that knowledge, especially to young adults.

Does it matter? What harm does it do to smoke a little pot or have a few beers? What is it like to be intoxicated? How long does it last? Will it make me feel really fine? Will it make me sick? What are the risks? These are but a few of the questions answered in this series, which, hopefully, will enable the reader to make wise decisions concerning the crucial issue of drugs.

Information sensibly acted upon can go a long way towards helping everyone develop his or her best self. As one keen and sensitive observer, Dr. Lewis Thomas, has said,

> *There is nothing at all absurd about the human condition. We matter. It seems to me a good guess, hazarded by a good many people who have thought about it, that we may be engaged in the formation of something like a mind for the life of this planet. If this is so, we are still at the most primitive stage, still fumbling with language and thinking, but infinitely capacitated for the future. Looked at this way, it is remarkable that we've come as far as we have in so short a period, really no time at all as geologists measure time. We are the newest, the youngest, and the brightest thing around.*

A pipe, scale, spirit lamp, and a violin-shaped case are all paraphernalia that can be used by opium smokers. On the other hand, heroin, a derivative of the opium poppy, is almost always taken by injection.

A 17th-century engraving depicts a man in Eastern dress collecting opium juice from the buds of poppy plants. Opium's painkilling, calming, and sleep-inducing properties were probably recognized as early as 3300 B.C.

CHAPTER 1

POPPIES AND POPULATIONS: A BRIEF HISTORY

Heroin is a drug derived from the opium poppy, *Papaver somniferum*, which means "the poppy that brings sleep." This name, however, hardly describes the many ways in which the extracts from the poppy affect human beings.

Opium's calming, painkilling, and sleep-inducing properties were first recognized more than 4,000 years ago and its use in medicine continues today. At one time, it was thought to bring courage to soldiers going into battle. Economies and trade routes were based on opium supply, and wars between nations in the East and West were fought because of it. Poets claiming to have gained visionary powers from opium have composed rich and lyrical verse. The accounts of opium users, however, also reveal the great suffering, unbearable addiction, and death caused by this powerful drug. Bold and often unsound claims, in the guise of scientific fact, have often been made about opium.

First synthesized in 1898 from morphine (a drug derived from opium), heroin was thought to be a safe means of curtailing or curing morphine addiction. In fact, Bayer, the company known for manufacturing aspirin, gave its version of the new product the name Heroin and began an intense, though brief, marketing campaign near the end of the 19th century. Heroin was included in medications such as cough suppressants and its potential for abuse was largely ignored.

It was many years before civil and medical authorities began to control the drug's distribution. This is because the economics of opium and its highly publicized and, to some degree, successful use in medicine (for example, to induce sleep in babies who have colic, or stomach irritation, and to bring relief from intense pain) colored people's perception of the drug, as did a number of naive theories and claims about the nature of heroin addiction. Since then a great deal of scientific data has accumulated, and today it is known that addiction to heroin has caused and continues to cause tremendous misery around the world.

The Early Use of Opium

Archaeological evidence suggests that more than 5,000 years ago in Mesopotamia (the area that is now Iraq), the Sumerians treated many ills with medicines made from the poppy. Later, the Assyrians and then the Babylonians inherited the art of slitting the flowering bulb of the poppy plant to collect and dry the milky juices, using the seed capsules to prepare potions. The ancient Egyptians called their opium preparations *thebacium* because the highly potent poppies used to make them grew near the capital city of Thebes. Egyptian priest-physicians praised the magic of the poppy and its household use spread throughout their civilization. The poppy's importance was so great that pharaohs were even entombed with opium artifacts at their sides. When Egyptian and Phoenician traders sailed across the Mediterranean to Greece and Rome, they brought the mysterious poppy with them. Often regarded as a gift of the gods, opium was mentioned in many myths and epics from these ancient cultures.

Hippocrates, the Greek physician who is generally recognized as the father of modern medicine, was one of the first people to describe the medicinal use of opium. He prescribed it frequently, and thereby helped establish practices that physicians would follow for 2,400 years. Galen, a Greek physician who practiced in the Roman Empire in the 2nd century, standardized the preparation of opium, creating a recipe called *mithridate*.

The poppy is technically an herb. White- or purple-petaled, the opium poppy is difficult to cultivate and grows best in moderate or warm climates. The process of collecting and preparing the plant's gummy juices is quite laborious. For these reasons, ancient peoples either ate parts of the flower or made them into liquids for drinking. By the 7th century, the Turkish and Islamic cultures of western Asia, however, had discovered that the drug's most powerful effects were produced by igniting and smoking the poppy's congealed juices. The Turks succeeded in cultivating larger crops. Arab merchants, who traded with peoples in the Far East, provided an economic incentive for the Turkish poppy cultivation by introducing the plant into these new markets. People in India and China soon began drinking or eating mild opium potions to ease the pain of minor ailments.

As early as the 11th century, Islamic doctors, the most advanced physicians of the premodern world, noted that the more opium a person took, the more he or she needed to take to gain the same effects experienced previously (an indication that an individual's body has become *tolerant* to the effects of the drug). By the 14th century, Arab scientists observed that continued use of the drug "degenerates," "corrupts," and "weakens the mind." It was already common knowledge that a single overdose could lead to death.

In Europe, opium use declined under the strong influence of the medieval Catholic church, which had strict doctrines about medicine. Then, in the early 16th century,

The ancient Greek physician Hippocrates, one of the first people to write about a medicinal use for opium, established practices that physicians would follow for well over 2,000 years. Hippocrates argued that diet, lifestyle, and environment should be considered when treating illness.

Paracelsus, a brilliant and unconventional Swiss physician and chemist, created a concoction known as *laudanum*, whose principal ingredient was opium. Paracelsus claimed that the drug could cure, not just ease, any pain-producing disease. He even insisted that laudanum could rejuvenate those who were close to death. Paracelsus and his followers attracted wide attention, and throughout the Western world laudanum gradually became one of the most popular and abused medications of all time. Even so, in Europe the availability of strong opium was limited until the 18th century, when increases in trade ushered in a new era.

The Growth of Opium Use

Authorized by the British Crown to advance English trade in India and the Far East, the British East India Company, a private commercial firm, began to make huge profits as the popularity of opium grew throughout southeastern Asia. In

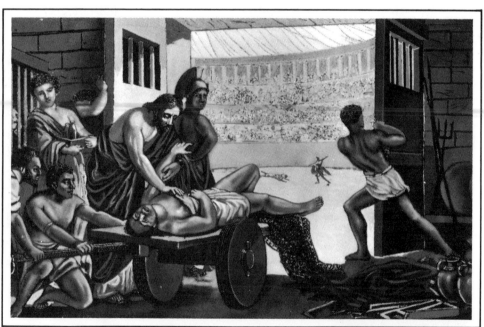

The physician Galen, appointed to care for the Roman gladiators, was a follower of Hippocratic theories of medicine and treated his patients with a preparation of opium called mithridate.

some ways, the British merely brought new life to a well-established market originally created by the Arab traders. In fact, by the time the Europeans arrived in India in the 16th century, in some cities "Take your opium" was a standard greeting.

Strongly held religious beliefs and cultural values in India were in conflict with the widespread use and frequent abuse of opium. But the appeal of the drug was so great that for millions of people in the Far East it proved irresistible — a fact that was not lost upon powerful Western companies. The Chinese imperial court vacillated over whether and how to control the growing use of opium, and it was no match for the aggressive traders who were supplying the drug.

During the 18th century, the British acquired an opium habit of their own. Ships from India supplied chemists and pharmacists all over Great Britain with literally tons of the drug. Countless varieties of new opium-based wonder drugs appeared everywhere, as did all kinds of publications that praised their virtues. The opium suppliers and merchants were hard at work in a riotous free market, each promoting his own supposedly superior products. As the 18th century drew to a close, one or more of the competing opium products could be found in virtually every British home.

There were physicians and scientists who could see the dangers of the excessive use of opium, but it was difficult to document social health problems at that time, so the dangers went unpublicized. The result was that neither the general public nor the authorities saw much cause for concern. Unlike alcohol, which even the ancient Romans knew could produce an uncontrollable and sometimes deadly craving in its users, opium was seen as a medicine. The very idea of addiction to a "cure" lacked a scientific basis in the biological and psychological theories of the day. Moreover, many of the people most actively investigating opium — physicians and chemists — were themselves frequent consumers of the drug. As a result, unbiased opinions on the issue were hard to come by. Also, the government itself had a large stake in the continued consumption of opium, since taxes on Indian exports and domestic imports accounted for a sizable part of British revenues. Opium, therefore, remained a cheap, plentiful, and readily available drug. These same conditions would exist in the United States in the 20th century.

"God's Own Medicine"

Having observed how poppy extracts varied greatly in their strength, Frederick Sertuerner, a German scientist, was determined to isolate the "specific narcotic elements of opium." In 1803 he derived from opium a crystal *alkaloid* (an organic compound that contains nitrogen) so potent that astonishingly small amounts produced powerful effects. Remembering Morpheus, the Greek god of dreams and sleep, Sertuerner called this chemical morphine. Within 20 years, morphine would begin to change the practice of medicine more quickly and dramatically than even opium had. And just as dramatically, it would transform the experience of drug addiction.

These transformations were made possible by the invention and refinement of the hypodermic syringe during the 1840s and 1850s. This device made it possible to administer morphine by injection, which guaranteed that the drug would be quickly absorbed into the bloodstream. As a result doctors — and, shortly thereafter, drug addicts — learned that injections into the veins brought extremely rapid and intense responses. Because injecting morphine required a degree of experience and skill, initially the practice was restricted to physicians, who were rapturous over the painkilling properties of the new drug. One leading British doctor went so far as to proclaim morphine "God's own medicine." By the middle of the 19th century morphine was being widely used throughout Europe and the United States to ease every kind of discomfort. In fact, the sales of this one drug helped establish some of the world's leading drug companies.

Amidst the enthusiasm, however, there were new warnings: the personal accounts of sadder but wiser opiate addicts. (The term opiate refers to the entire family of poppy-based drugs.) Although a century later there would be a cascade of such tales, the most celebrated account was that of the British writer Thomas De Quincey. His book, *Confessions of an English Opium-Eater*, published in 1822, engrossed both medical professionals and the reading public. It is the intimate narration of how his own medicinal use of laudanum was transformed into a euphoric pastime that went on to become a raging nightmare. The *Confessions* documented the phenomena of *tolerance* (how the use of a few drops of even a mild opiate tincture could swell to the need for pints of the substance); *denial* (how a chronic user would deceive him- or herself about the escalating abuse and dependence); and *withdrawal* (the unbearable agonies brought on by the cessation of drug use). Inadvertently De Quincey also opened the door to the use of laudanum and other opiates by a host of authors and poets during the 19th century, including Samuel Coleridge, Charles Baudelaire, Lord Byron, John Keats, Edgar Allan Poe, Elizabeth Barrett Browning, and Algernon Swinburne. But although they and other artists sometimes searched for creativity through opium, most 19th-century artists took the drug the way almost everyone did — as medicine. Pharmacies sold little vials of laudanum (and even candied opiates later in the century) by the thousands. It was cheaper than gin. The working class, upper class, the very young, the very old — nearly everyone took laudanum.

The Opium Wars

The big business of opium continued to thrive in the East. The habit of smoking raw opium had made its way up from India along the southeastern coast of China. Native poppy cultivation was also spreading. Although the British population enjoyed opium as a gift, the guardians of China's culture saw that opium wasted the lives of its smokers. It cost their nation silver and other trade commodities that it could ill

In the 19th century the British aggressively marketed India-grown opium. The quality, price, and destination of this crop were determined by men with strong commercial interests and expertise.

afford, and it humbled the ancient Central Kingdom (as China was then called) before the mercenary West. (The West included the Americans who, to the great displeasure of the British, smuggled Turkish opium into China.) The smoke from opium dens, where users gathered to enjoy their pipes in secret, drifted over the coastlines and even rose above inland cities. Even the emperor's court had its smokers, as did all levels within the government and the army. By 1820 more than 300 tons of pure opium were imported annually. Ten years later, even after officials attempted harsh restrictions, the figure approached 2,000 tons a year. It is estimated that millions of Chinese were addicted to opium.

The British government was still convinced that more profit was possible from the opium traders. It revoked the

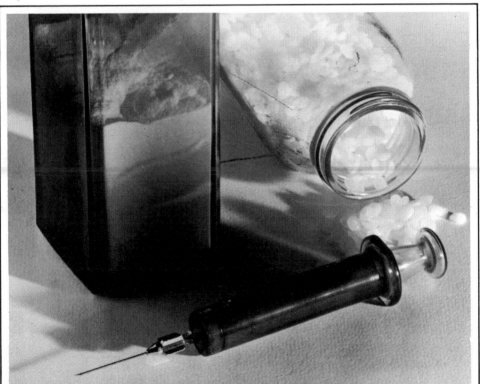

The hypodermic syringe, invented in the mid-1800s, revolutionized medical practice because it allowed precise administration of a drug by injection, resulting in quick absorption into the bloodstream.

charter of the British East India Company and acted directly to open Chinese ports to even more opium trade. The Chinese emperor was under strong pressure from his advisers to legalize opium. Although opium was still considered unsafe, the authorities hoped that through legislation, corruption and foreign influence could be minimized. But the emperor refused to legalize the drug. Instead, he began military preparations and ordered the executions of users and traffickers, foreign and domestic. The most notable effect of this policy was to anger the British. Within a year, the Opium War of 1839 began. When the Chinese lost the war three years later, they were forced to sign the Treaty of Nanking, which required them to pay large reparations and to surrender totally to British commercial interests. As a result, by 1852 opium imports had doubled. In 1856, with China under the rule of a new emperor, a second opium war began. This, however, brought China only more death, more reparations to pay, and more humiliation. Opium became officially legalized, and the Chinese ports were opened as never before to Western influences of every sort.

The Opium Wars have generated much analysis and historical commentary. Today many historians believe that opportunistic commercial interests had merely taken advantage of opium as a commodity — an especially insidious one to be sure — seeking any way to attain financial success. The clash between the expanding industrial powers of the West and the protective, tradition-bound culture of China might well have erupted eventually over some other commodity.

A Dope Fiend's Paradise

In the United States during this period, as in Britain, laudanum and similar opiate *tinctures* (alcoholic extracts) had become popular home remedies. Americans were even less inclined than the British to see opium's potential dangers. Indeed, between 1830 and 1870, when the land was awash with patent medicines, the United States' importation of opium increased twentyfold.

During the 1850s and 1860s tens of thousands of Chinese entered the United States to help build the western railroads and to work the California mines. They brought with them the practice of opium smoking. Besides being an integral part of Chinese lifestyle, opium smoking provided some measure of relief from the dirty, unhealthy, and physically demanding labor they performed. Thus, the United States came to know Chinese opium smoking firsthand as the opium dens of the West Coast became steadily more common and notorious.

Shortly after the Civil War, West Coast authorities, influenced by strong racist sentiments, enacted the nation's first anti-opium laws. The public's grossly distorted image of the addict was that of the predatory, godless, and depraved Oriental. One consequence of this view was that the public failed to recognize addiction among its white citizens, who never visited the Chinese "dens of iniquity" or smoked opium, but were addicted in other ways.

Further changing the course of opium use in the United States and abroad was the use of morphine — as both a painkiller and to combat dysentery — during times of war. Particularly in the American Civil War, and to a lesser extent in the European wars later in the 19th century, morphine was used so freely on the battlefield that its overuse became known as the "army disease." Only when many Civil War veterans became obviously dependent on morphine did American society as a whole suddenly become more familiar with the drug.

However, it was not just soldiers and patent medicine salesmen who spread the word about morphine's "miraculous" properties. In 1868 one of the country's leading medical textbooks described opiates in the following glowing terms:

> [Opiates] cause a feeling of delicious ease and comfort, with an elevation and expansion of the whole moral and intellectual nature.... There is not the same uncontrollable excitement as from alcohol, but an exaltation of our better mental qualities, a warmer glow of benevolence, a disposition to do great things, but nobly and beneficently, a higher devotional spirit, and withal a stronger self-reliance, and consciousness of power. Nor is this consciousness altogether mistaken. For the intellectual and imaginative faculties are raised to the highest point compatible with individual capacity.... Opium seems to make the individual, for a time, a better and greater man.

Who could resist such a "medicine"? And why *would* anyone resist it? Opiates were legal, abundant, and cheap. The mystery of how they actually worked within the body continued to evoke only vague and colorful speculation. Public opinion held that only people who were constitutionally weak in body or mind needed to abstain from opiates. As the last years of the 19th century approached, the United States was, in the words of one historian, a "dope fiend's paradise."

Changing Perceptions and New Realities

While opiates and other drugs (such as *cocaine*) were beginning to cause serious trouble in the United States, Britain's relatively stable society was being affected by a more moderate drug-consumption problem. Although there was not a large addict population in Britain, there was a pervasive, low-

Portrait of Thomas de Quincey, author of **Confessions of an English Opium-Eater.** *First published in 1822, and still in print, de Quincey's book tells of the unbearable agonies brought on by attempts to end a drug addiction.*

level addiction to laudanum-type medications, a problem that was seen as largely "medical." As British anti-opium groups began to agitate more strongly for reform at home as well as abroad, the sale of opiate products increasingly became restricted to pharmacies. At the same time, British moral reform groups, often led by overseas missionaries, were also becoming more aware of the opium problems in China and India. They expressed outrage and guilt about the Opium Wars and demanded an end to the opium trade. Slowly, opiate use among the British began to decrease.

In the United States there was a different atmosphere that contributed to an unprecedented increase in the abuse of opiates. Between 1880 and 1910 the U.S. population grew by 83%. Personal liberty was romanticized and often zealously guarded. Economic and social progress seemed to promise an end to all known ills and suffering. New fashions traveled

THE BETTMANN ARCHIVE

An engraving depicts an 1842 battle during the Opium War between China and Britain. Fearing the devastating effects of opium on his people, the Chinese emperor fought a losing battle to stop its importation.

from coast to coast at unheard-of speed, and there was a great desire to be up to date. One of the most up-to-date fashions was opiate use, and the amount of imported opium rose dramatically during the late 1800s. During this period, in Iowa alone, a state still relatively free of opium dens and big-city vices, sales of over-the-counter opiated medicines jumped by 700%. In 1883 such products were sold in more than 3,000 stores. In its 1897 mail-order catalogue, Sears, Roebuck, and Company then offered a selection of hypodermic syringe kits. An individual could easily obtain morphine at any pharmacy, and a few years later, heroin became available. By 1906 there were 50,000 different patent medicines containing opiates.

The principal consumers of patent medicines were middle- and upper-class people, mainly older women in the northeast and white males in the south. Many customers took these remedies on a regular high-dose basis; others consumed low doses of relatively mild formulas constantly over long periods, apparently without ill effects. But among many people in every walk of life there began to appear some classic symptoms: insomnia, moodiness, depression, loss of concentration, chronic constipation, an obsessive need for one's "medicine," and intense physical illness whenever drug use was abruptly discontinued.

In newspapers, popular magazines, and professional journals, sensationalized personal stories of the horror of addiction began to appear. Yet many physicians continued to praise and prescribe narcotics. Others, however, were quicker to notice the telltale signs of addiction and began to write about "morphinism," "narcomania," and the "disease" of the "opium appetite." Administering morphine by injection warranted special concern. One eminent physician wrote, "There is no proceeding in medicine that has become so rapidly popular . . . so great a blessing, and so great a curse." Opiate addiction in the United States was becoming all too obvious. In 1920 New York City officials reported that in their city alone 300,000 people were "hooked" on morphine or the new scourge, heroin.

Public awareness of the problem came slowly and unevenly. Many newspapers in the western United States blamed the relatively small population of Chinese laborers for spreading addiction. Sensationalist "yellow journalism" and racism were used to publicize the issue. Even the progressive labor leader Samuel Gompers, "Father of American Labor Unions," wrote emotional tracts that linked opium smoking and "coolie" (Chinese) labor to a coming social catastrophe. He wrote about American youths who had to "yield up their virgin bodies to their maniacal yellow captors" and said that "our American girls and boys who have acquired this deathly habit opium smoking are doomed, hopelessly doomed." In reality, the boom-and-bust conditions in San Francisco and other western cities where the Chinese lived had generated all the gambling, prostitution, and other forms of vice necessary to attract wayward youths.

For a while, marijuana (then usually called hashish) and cocaine were also used in some patent medicines. But neither drug had the established market or the unique medical value of opium. After 1900, their use seemed to be more common among southern blacks, bohemian whites, and others who often found themselves either in conflict with or the targets of conventional attitudes. These groups helped to establish the networks through which opiates would flow most easily in later years. Like the Chinese, these groups were easy targets and thus became the scapegoats for the social hostility that went hand-in-hand with the 20th-century attack on all drugs.

In the United States in the late 1800s, moral reform movements provided the momentum for a revised outlook toward drugs. Religious fundamentalist groups sought to preserve pre-Civil War values and social norms against the incursions of industrialization and the influence of new immigrants and freed slaves. Progressive reformers spoke out against corruption in politics and big business. And the temperance movement's crusade against "demon" alcohol was gaining in importance. These various movements had a great influence on American society, and gradually their moralistic messages began to include anti-opiate sentiments.

In 1898, as one of the spoils of the Spanish-American War, the United States acquired the Philippines and thus became the protector of a large population that included many opium users. Just as England had a foreign drug problem, the United States now had one too. In addition, many Americans believed that soldiers sent to the Philippines risked becoming addicted. Calls for controls on the distribution of opium were sounded as nations around the world came to see how difficult it was to limit use of the drug.

Meanwhile, a new drug appeared on the scene. In 1874 the British chemist C. R. Wright synthesized *diacetylmorphine* from morphine. But the substance did not become known to physicians or the general public in the United States until almost 25 years later. In 1898 Heinrich Dreser, a chemist who helped develop aspirin, also synthesized diacetylmorphine. Dreser, however, was backed by his employer, the Bayer Company. Finding the new medicine more potent than morphine, and apparently less apt to produce nausea, constipation, and the other side effects of the opiates, Bayer promoted it as a singularly effective cough suppressant. Soon, however, company researchers discovered that this new drug produced the same dependence that was associated with morphine. In fact, diacetylmorphine did so more quickly than any other opiate. Bayer immediately stopped promoting di-

An opium den in New York City's Chinatown. Opiate addiction had become a serious problem by the 1920s, and many Americans unjustly blamed the small Chinese population for its use.

acetylmorphine, but continued to distribute it. Although the drug never became a stock item on store shelves, it remained legally available for a generation. This was enough time for much less sophisticated laboratories around the world to learn how to reproduce Wright's and Dreser's new medicine and make famous the trade name Bayer had given it — Heroin.

Attempts to Cure and Control Opiate Addiction

Opiate addiction was officially recognized as early as the 11th century. Cures that involved alchemy, sorcery, and herbal antidotes were all attempted, but none achieved any notable success. Not surprisingly, as addiction increased in the 19th century the search for a cure gained momentum. But the question remained: Who needed to be cured, and of what exactly were they to be cured? Most users of mildly opiated home remedies showed no ill effects as long as they had enough of their "medicine." The popular view was that there were really two kinds of addicts. The first type was the deviant who, because he or she belonged to an "inferior" race and/

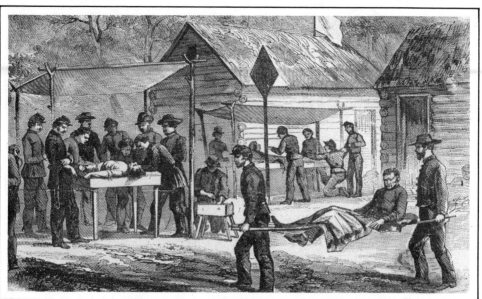

THE BETTMANN ARCHIVE

The extensive administration of morphine as both a painkiller and a relief for dysentery during the American Civil War altered the patterns of opium use throughout the rest of the 19th century.

or had a defective personality, took drugs as a wicked pleasure, with little concern for the consequences. The second
type of addict was the good but unfortunate citizen whose
problems were a result of unintentional overuse of medicinal
opiates. This distinction, reinforced by the press and other
organizations, was entirely misleading and disguised the true
nature of addiction.

Another popular misconception was that discontinuing
opiate use could lead directly to death. Although most physicians knew this outcome was unlikely and, in fact, almost
unheard of, when they encountered a patient whose habit
was out of control, they rarely advised abstinence. Instead,
they would recommend some other opiate that they considered safer or administer other drugs such as *belladonna*.

Belladonna, known since ancient times as an herbal medicine extracted from the poisonous plant *Atropa belladonna*,
is a nonaddicting but very powerful mood-altering tranquilizer that affects the central nervous system. The chemicals
in belladonna were thought to help purge opiates from the
stomach and the intestinal tract. This purge therapy was supported by contemporary theories that addiction would end
if the body could be fully rid of opiate "toxins," or poisons.
By the turn of the century, throughout the United States and
Europe, purge therapy had become a big business.

Countless quicker, cheaper, and less painful "cures"
were also highly popular. Most of these were simply disguised
opiates that allowed addicts to think, at least for a day or so,
that their *detoxification* (a gradual to rapid weaning from
opiate use), had been painless. There were also claims that
other remedies, including largely unaided withdrawals in
confined sanitariums, were successful. "Cure clinics" reported that 90% of their patients were completely withdrawn
from drugs.

Such encouraging assertions, however, could not be supported by hard facts. In fact, most patients, even those who
had gone to the most "successful" sanitariums, ended up
returning to opiate use, usually within six months of their
"cure." Even addicts who were desperate for a cure often
readmitted themselves to clinics because they could not stay
away from opiates. Scientists did not understand why this
behavior pattern occurred. They discovered no toxins or
chemical clues that could explain the relapses. Doctors were

at a loss and could recommend only continued moderate use of opiates. For the "bad" addicts, who did not seek medical help (which frequently only the wealthy could afford), even harder times were to come.

Cure specialists continued to promote their techniques with great energy. In addition, the belief that cures were available convinced lawmakers that opiates could be used safely if their distribution was restricted. With San Francisco taking the lead in enacting local ordinances, in the 1870s California and the other western states began to limit the sale of raw opium and enacted other measures, usually pointedly anti-Chinese, to prohibit opium smoking. In 1883 and again in 1890, the United States Congress raised the tariffs on opium prepared for smoking, and in 1909 it completely banned the importation of opium. Unfortunately, as a result of the new restrictions, drug smuggling and illicit distribution increased. Newly formed criminal organizations, called "tongs" in the Chinese community, trafficked in opium, and in the process caused an unprecedented degree of corruption and violence.

The drug companies and their merchandisers fought to keep processed opiates available. They did, however, consent to the federal Pure Food and Drug Act of 1906, which required that opiated patent medicines carry labels listing their ingredients. Informed about what their remedies really contained, many Americans chose to reduce their opiate consumption sharply.

Sparked by President Theodore Roosevelt's antinarcotics adviser, Dr. Hamilton Wright, the first of two international conferences was held in Shanghai in 1909. Out of this conference came a statement regarding the Western concern about opium addiction in China and the vow of all conference participants to begin a worldwide effort to restrict the distribution of narcotics. The second conference, The Hague Convention of 1912, made specific recommendations to further the goals announced in Shanghai.

These gatherings further spurred the efforts of U.S. authorities to solve their country's own opiate problems. In 1914 Congress passed the Harrison Act. On the surface a tax on opiates, it actually sought to restrict dramatically the distribution of narcotics and cocaine (but *not* heroin, which Congress did not yet know to be addictive) and limit even physicians' prescribing powers.

The Heroin Addict as Criminal

The Harrison Act, along with a host of similar laws, judicial rulings, and enforcement practices, brought rapid decreases both in the consumption of opiates and in the number of consumers. As a consequence, the incidence of new addictions was also reduced. These laws also caused tens of thousands of people who were only marginally addicted to stop using opiates. The impact on true opiate addiction, however, was another matter. The authorities who promoted the Harrison Act believed that there were cures for addiction, but, in fact, these "cures" usually consisted only of detoxification and even these "cures" were available only to those who could afford to enter private clinics. As a result, most detoxified individuals relapsed within months, and poorer addicts were seldom treated at all. In addition, within a year after New York State banned other opiates in 1913, almost all the addicts in New York City had turned to heroin. With the imposition of the Harrison Act, a similar phenomenon occurred nationwide.

An 1862 photograph of the ambulance corps that was organized shortly after the Battle of Antietam. Morphine was prescribed so freely during the Civil War that its overuse became known as the "army disease."

THE BETTMANN ARCHIVE

Chemically more potent and, to many addicts, more euphoric than morphine, heroin did not need to be injected; a user could snort, or sniff, it. Congress finally became aware of the problem, and in 1924 federal law made the use of heroin illegal.

The criminalization of opiates had far-ranging social consequences. Indeed, in 1919 the United States Supreme Court ruled that the Harrison Act forbade even doctors from authorizing long-term, or maintenance, doses for deeply dependent users — no matter what the origin of the dependence was. So vigorous was the enforcement effort that within 10 years of its formation, the Bureau of Narcotics had arrested 25,000 physicians and twice as many drug users. The old distinction between "good" and "bad" addicts was rapidly breaking down.

An engraving depicts an anti-Chinese riot during the 1880s. During this era, the Chinese were the victims of severe and sometimes violent racism. They were accused of being the only group that smoked opium; this convenient delusion allowed white citizens to ignore the drug addiction that was rampant within their own community.

THE BETTMANN ARCHIVE

Public anti-narcotics campaigns stressed the criminality of addiction, claiming that heroin was "the most crime inspiring of all drugs" and that its users became "insane" and "bloodthirsty." Caught up in the pervasive fear of foreign powers and internal subversives that existed during the period surrounding World War I, American politicians, newspaper editors, veterans' organizations, local police, and countless other voices of "patriotism" and "order" spread the rumor that "dope fiends" (heroin addicts) brought anarchy and sedition, were enslaved by the "German invention," were Bolsheviks (communists), and constituted a national menace.

The idea that heroin itself inspired crime or that it was the drug preferred by hardened criminals had little basis in fact. What *was* true was that during the same period when heroin was replacing other opiates, addicts were beginning to be prosecuted for the use and possession of drugs. The addict population was also becoming younger and more urban. The suppliers could now operate most profitably in the cities and, as opiates were now viewed as a forbidden and alluring vice of the adult world, more young people began to use drugs. City youth gangs were growing. They tended to attract young men who were newcomers to the city, often unemployed and disillusioned, burdened with large amounts of free time and eager for some excitement. Racist stereotypes of addicts returned once again, but this time the blacks rather than the Chinese were the targets. Many misinformed people thought that blacks, who had already been unfairly linked with cocaine abuse and its consequences, were very likely to rape and assault under the influence of heroin.

New criminal organizations appeared and replaced the Chinese tongs' role in drug trafficking. They owed their existence in part to Prohibition — the 18th Amendment to the U.S. Constitution, passed in 1919 — which made alcoholic beverages illegal in the United States and inadvertently made bootlegging (the illegal production or sale of alcohol) a very big business. Although it would be years before the bootleggers would turn their attention from alcohol to heroin (Prohibition, a failed experiment, was finally repealed in 1933), the black market in narcotics was already taking shape by the 1920s. Using the black market as one's source of heroin meant paying much higher prices, depending on an uncertain supply, using adulterated drugs (drugs mixed with impurities), and dealing with unsavory associates — all of which made addiction a more desperate and dangerous lifestyle.

Recognizing that help was needed, between 1919 and 1920 the federal government authorized several dozen outpatient clinics in cities across the country to "cure" addicts who had no other resources. The addicts were detoxified through daily decreasing doses of morphine or heroin. Bitter controversies erupted surrounding charges that the clinics were *maintaining*, not *detoxifying*, their patients, and that several facilities were poorly controlled and corruptly managed. Within a year, this notable effort at government-sponsored treatment was stopped, and all the clinics were forced to close. As a result, their 15,000 patients (and all the other addicts around the country) were left with few choices. If they could afford a doctor's services, they could get professional help; otherwise they either detoxified on their own or remained on the streets, where they continued to buy and use illegal drugs, a practice that frequently led to arrest and imprisonment, illness, or death from an overdose.

A WORD OF CAUTION TO OUR FRIENDS, THE CIGAR-MAKERS.
Through the smoke it is easy to see the approach of Chinese cheap labor.

Trade unions, fearful of competing against cheap Chinese labor, supported restrictions against Chinese immigration during the l870s and 1880s. This cartoon warns cigar makers not to use Chinese labor.

THE BETTMANN ARCHIVE

Different, more moderate trends continued in Great Britain. Controls on the importation of narcotics had steadily reduced the supply, and the medical profession had kept effective primary authority over the dispensing of opiates. In 1926 a major commission reaffirmed the long-held British position that "with few exceptions, addiction to morphine and heroin should be regarded as a manifestation of a morbid [that is, diseased] state and not as a mere form of vicious indulgence." Indeed, for the next 40 years the street addict who would come to loom so large on the American scene was rare in Great Britain, where most addicts received morphine on doctors' orders and under close medical supervision. Only in the 1960s did the British once again have serious problems with illegal opiates and other drugs. By then, other Europeans were also confronting widespread narcotics abuse.

The British eventually adopted a system that required confirmed addicts to register as such, whereupon they could receive regular doses of morphine or heroin from authorized clinics or doctors. It is still a controversial approach (most policies regarding drug addiction are), but within the context of the nation's population, culture, and past experiences with opiate use, it has worked relatively well.

In the 20th century, the Far East has had even greater success than the West battling its opiate problem. Strong internal and international pressures brought an end to the large-scale importation of opium to China. And, though addiction and associated corruption continued into the 1930s, as national concerns they were overshadowed by the military and political upheavals of this revolutionary period. Mao Zedong's People's Republic of China brought a drastic conclusion to what remained of the old opium culture.

India, for so long the major grower of high-quality poppies, managed a particularly benign control and reduction of the opium supply. However, addiction rates had always remained relatively low in this country, at least partly because of British supervision of cultivation and the traditional practice of using mild opiates primarily for medicinal and culturally approved purposes. As Indians assumed greater authority, and eventually achieved self-rule in 1947, they worked systematically and successfully to reduce both the cultivation and the use of opium by promoting traditional religious and moral values, which opposed intoxication. By the time Europe and America saw the use of heroin resurfacing among the young, addiction was nearly extinct in India, where the few opium addicts still living were mainly middle-aged or older. The decreased use of opiates in India and China began before either nation had significant exposure to morphine or heroin.

The American "dope fiend" began to fade from the headlines during the 1920s and the 1930s. Although the Bureau of Narcotics reported that its efforts had decreased drug use, in fact addiction was merely becoming more covert — addicts were forced to remain underground and more frequently identified by the crimes they had to commit to pay for heroin. Heroin was the perfect black market drug because it was much easier and much more profitable to refine it overseas and ship small bags of its odorless powder through customs than it was to smuggle in large cargoes of raw, odorous opium. Because local distribution rings needed to avoid detection, they began to operate principally in poorer sections of large cities, where secret deals with the poor, young, urban drug users could be made most easily. Only those addicts who had special connections or who were medical professionals managed to avoid the life of the heroin underworld. (There were more than a few addicts in both categories. Among the medical professionals was Dr. William Halsted, who, though a secret and heavy morphine addict until his death, was a pioneer in modern surgery and helped establish the Johns Hopkins Medical School.)

Although heroin addicts were popularly portrayed as willful criminals, there were still physicians who were determined to discover a real cure — some way to end addiction other than by cutting off the supply of narcotics, which was rarely successful. In 1935 Congress allowed a new kind of corrections program to start in Lexington, Kentucky. At that facility, which was a large, farmlike complex, convicted addicts were to be studied carefully and humanely and, as a pressing practical matter, admitted in numbers large enough to partially relieve the overburdened federal prisons. At the Addiction Research Center component of the new facility, physicians and scientists would for the first time be able to apply systematic research to the phenomenon of opiate addiction. Treatment included gradual detoxification using morphine and, for several months thereafter, voluntary psychiatric counseling and work training. Although the center never claimed a cure rate of more than 15%, through the 1950s its many distinguished researchers produced innovative studies of the physiology, psychology, and behaviors of addiction. These studies form the basis of many present-day treatment techniques and current understanding about morphine addiction.

Ironically, but not for the first time, treatment research produced new addicting drugs. The Lexington center, in its search for new, safe painkillers, synthesized opiatelike substances that would eventually become widely prescribed by doctors and widely abused by both hard-core heroin addicts and less experienced users.

In many cities in the western United States, Chinese laborers were blamed for corrupting American youth. Chinese immigrants were thoroughly searched for opium when they arrived in San Francisco.

For the nation as a whole at mid-century, the drug problem seemed to be quieting down. The efforts of Harry Anslinger, longtime head of the Bureau of Narcotics, and other enforcement officials certainly played a part. In addition, World War II disrupted smuggling operations and diverted most opium to the medical needs of war victims all over the globe. By the end of the war, it was estimated that there were fewer than 50,000 heroin addicts in the United States.

Although some people still associated heroin with foreign subversion, such as the new "Red Menace" of the Soviet Union, most Americans had come to see it as the scourge of urban blacks, prostitutes, jazz musicians, bohemian artists, and criminal psychopaths — all inhabitants of America's evil underworld that no "decent" citizen would want or need to enter. Such characterizations served to keep addicts and addiction at a safe mental distance. However, after the war years there were enough unemployed and disillusioned people and enough readily obtainable heroin to renew a wider market. While narcotics agents continued their long-standing practice of going after the individual users and dealers (users often became small-time dealers to support their own habits), large crime organizations were exploiting the new market. By the late 1950s, there were approximately 100,000 heroin addicts in the United States.

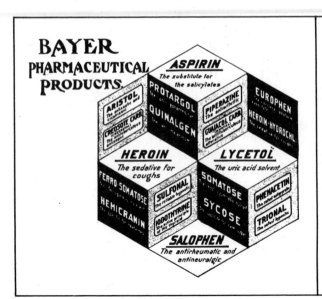

At the turn of the century, countless varieties of new "wonder drugs" appeared everywhere accompanied by extravagant and invalid claims about their effectiveness. By 1906 there were some 50,000 different brands of opiated formulas on the American market.

In the 1960s, the youthful counterculture swept the nation. It was a time of unconventional fashions and anti-establishment attitudes. In unprecedented numbers, middle- and upper-class people experimented with illegal drugs to get high. They smoked marijuana; tried the new synthetic hallucinogens such as LSD; discovered the psychoactive properties of amphetamines and barbiturates; rediscovered the almost forgotten product of the coca plant, cocaine; and, for the first time, people from the mainstream of American life began to experiment with derivatives of the opium poppy. Thus, heroin addiction made its insidious way back to the forefront of national concern.

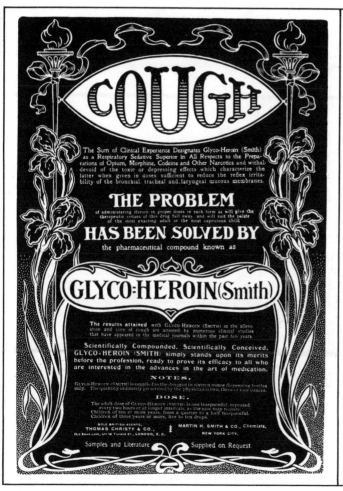

This 1903 advertisement for Glyco-Heroin promotes the medicinal properties that were ascribed to heroin. Some people mistakenly believed that the drug was also a cure for morphine addiction.

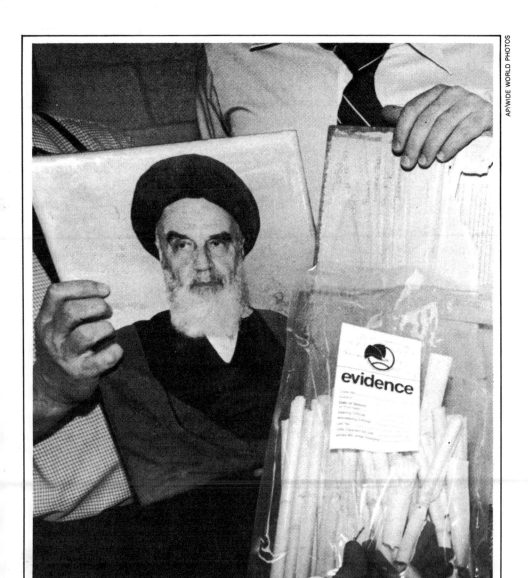

A plastic bag contains opium smuggled into the United States inside pictures of Iran's Ayatollah Ruhollah Khomeini. As little as $500 of raw opium can be converted into $2 million of street heroin.

CHAPTER 2

HEROIN ADDICTION IN THE MODERN WORLD

*H*eroin is more expensive than opium. It takes 10 tons of opium to produce one ton of heroin. But opium producers do not have to export much to supply the world market. The entire U.S. addict population uses approximately five tons a year, representing only about 2.5% of the annual world production of illegal opium. Fewer than 10 square miles of poppy fields can supply the entire U.S. market. The remainder goes to the millions of addicts around the world who are tending to switch from opium to heroin.

Estimating the number of heroin addicts worldwide is difficult for two reasons. First, governments would often prefer to deny or minimize the problem of heroin addiction. Second, addiction is by nature a hidden phenomenon. However, the following facts indicate the extent and character of heroin addiction:

There were an estimated 600,000 to 700,000 addicts in the United States in 1985, most of them living in urban areas. Almost a third of the addict population lives in New York City. About 40% are white, 40% are black, and the rest, a growing proportion, are Hispanic and Oriental. Typically, the U.S. addict is a male in his twenties who started using heroin in his late teens. Approximately one-quarter of all heroin addicts are female. Most, but by no means all, addicts are poor. In 1980 an estimated 8,700 people died of heroin overdose.

Thailand has about as many addicts as the United States, and its largest city, Bangkok, may have 400,000 addicts — almost twice the number estimated to be in New York City.

Italy has 200,000 heroin addicts, who represent a larger percentage of the population than they do in the United States.

Pakistan had virtually no heroin addicts in 1979. But by 1985, the country reportedly had more than 150,000 heroin addicts in addition to its opium users.

In recent years, West Germany has reported almost as many deaths attributable to heroin overdose as the United States has.

Several hundred thousand addicts, at a minimum, populate the nations of Malaysia and the Philippines in eastern Asia.

Major cities throughout Mexico and other Latin American countries have serious heroin addiction problems, as do cities in Africa. There is evidence that heroin use is again on the rise in India and even, some observers have said, in China.

Heroin addiction has reportedly been increasing even in the communist bloc nations of Czechoslovakia, Poland, and Bulgaria.

Somewhere in Turkey, women sow opium poppy seeds. The legal production of opium for the manufacture of medicines is a carefully controlled agricultural industry in both India and Turkey.

UPI/BETTMANN NEWSPHOTOS

There are countries that have avoided significant problems with heroin, however. One notable example is the Soviet Union, although it has high rates of alcoholism and has recently shown signs of other substance abuse. Even some countries that are nearer to Asian opium sources, such as Japan, South Korea, and Taiwan, have escaped large-scale addiction. Political controls or strong cultural taboos and patterns have seemed to effectively prevent opiate use in these nations. But as international travel increases and exposure to other cultures expands, it is unlikely that any nation can remain immune to the spread of drug abuse and addiction.

Worldwide Opium Production and Consumption

Today the legal production of opium for the purpose of manufacturing codeine, morphine, and other opium-based medications is a carefully controlled agricultural industry. India is still the leader in this industry, having ended illegal pro-

REUTERS/BETTMANN NEWSPHOTOS

A Pakistani man measures out heroin in his shop. The number of heroin addicts in Pakistan ballooned to 150,000 in 1985, a dramatic increase since 1975, when there were virtually no Pakistani users of the drug.

duction of opium at the beginning of the 20th century. Currently, Turkey is the second largest grower of legal opium poppies, and smaller quantities are legally grown in a number of other nations, mostly in Europe.

Turkey's illegal suppliers were cut off from their markets when the infamous French Connection smuggling organization, which shipped through the French port of Marseilles, was broken up in the early 1970s. Illegal poppy cultivation is still rampant, however, in the area of southeastern Asia known as the Golden Triangle and in the nations that make up the Golden Crescent in southwestern Asia.

Opium from the Golden Triangle countries — Burma, Thailand, and Laos — became the principal source of the world's heroin after the illegal Turkish trade ended. The war in Vietnam also contributed to the development of the black

REUTERS/BETTMANN NEWSPHOTOS

Mexican troops leap from a government helicopter in search of illegal poppy and marijuana fields. In 1985, approximately one-third of the heroin smuggled into the United States came from Mexico.

market trade in that region. The war severely disrupted political institutions, government controls, and traditional family and community structures. Thousands of U.S. servicemen
were comparatively rich, and perhaps naive, new drug customers. Profiteers, always ready to exploit the chaos of war,
began to smuggle heroin out of the region. By the mid-1970s,
U.S. addicts had found another major source, Mexico. Coarse,
brown-colored heroin was refined from new opium fields in
Mexico's mountains and valleys.

Heroin markets grew significantly in the United States
and Western Europe until 1978, when severe drought hit the
crops of the Golden Triangle. Mexican authorities cooperated
with the U.S. and responded quickly to wipe out many of the
Mexican opium fields with commercial defoliants. As a result,
the addict population in the United States fell from an esti-

A Mexican soldier in an anti-drug brigade collects illegal poppy plants in Sinaloa. In 1986 United States officials escalated their criticism of the Mexican government for its seeming inability to control drug trafficking.

mated 750,000 to less than 500,000. Soon, however, heroin was being imported from the Golden Crescent, where political turmoil made legal and social controls ineffective. In 1980 the region produced an estimated 1,300 tons of raw opium.

The countries of the Golden Triangle and the Golden Crescent continue to undergo powerful social and political stresses, and there is no telling what their impact will be on future opium production. But it is thought that huge opium stockpiles have been hidden away in both regions. In addition, Mexican production has risen again; in 1985 it accounted for approximately one-third of the heroin used in the United States. Barring drastic change, the world will remain amply supplied with heroin for many years.

Why Opium Production Continues

Almost all governments want heroin use ended, and even officials in the nations that supply the drug strongly oppose the opium market. Why are they unable to get rid of the illegal poppy fields?

An opium grower harvests the spring crop in northwest Pakistan. Although it takes 10 tons of opium to produce 1 ton of heroin, fewer than 10 square miles of poppy fields can provide enough of the drug to supply all the heroin addicts in the United States for an entire year.

AP/WIDE WORLD PHOTOS

Huge amounts of opium continue to be cultivated for many reasons. For one thing, opium is a long-established part of many native cultures. Serious political, cultural, or ethnic divisions make it extremely difficult for the central governments of supplier nations to maintain control within their own borders. For example, in Iran, government leaders try to exert absolute authority. Yet, discontented minorities, such as the Kurds, bitterly fight the government's control. The Kurdish minority grows, uses, and smuggles large quantities of opium out of Iran. The Lao people represent a similar challenge to the authorities in Laos. Profits from opium may even finance wars against the central government itself, as in Afghanistan, where rebel forces smuggle the drug across the mountains to Pakistan in exchange for arms to fight the Soviet-backed regime.

But the major problem seems to be that all the countries where opium poppies are grown are poor. Opium brings growers and laborers more money than almost any other crop, sometimes three to five times more, and it is easier to grow. The desperately poor peasants who tend poppy fields

AP/WIDE WORLD PHOTOS

Workers use a saw-toothed instrument to cut open poppy capsules. Inside the plant is raw opium, which is a milky juice before being dried in the sun and processed into heroin.

are unwilling to give up their profits even though their product causes pain and suffering throughout the world. The local middlemen who organize the growing and smuggling make even more money; sometimes they are government officials who secretly sabotage their own government's efforts to crack down on illegal drug traffic. Even if an illegal operation is stopped, the principal drug traffickers can usually start up new operations elsewhere, enticing growers and laborers with ready cash.

The Black Market

Opium is typically grown in remote areas that are usually far removed from government power centers by mountains and deserts. With good weather and the best growing conditions, each acre of poppies yields approximately 10 kg (kilogram; 1 kg is equal to 2.2 lb) of opium. From a local buyer, the

Two Afghan rebels share a mount during a raid against Soviet troops in 1980. Rebel forces have smuggled opium across the mountains to Pakistan in exchange for arms to fight the Soviet-backed regime.

UPI/BETTMANN NEWSPHOTOS

villagers may receive in advance the equivalent of a few hundred dollars per acre, tax-free. Either near the harvest site or in a well-protected location, each 10 kg of opium is refined to 1 kg of morphine, which can be easily transported. The morphine is further refined into 1 kg of heroin either at a regional laboratory, which may be only a simple shed or workroom, or at a more distant facility in another country. Each kilogram of the morphine or heroin that has been smuggled out of the remote countryside represents several thousand dollars in market value.

Because of the remote location of the poppy fields, soldiers and police cannot easily locate or get to them to destroy the opium. But growers can smuggle small bags of opium by pack animal or on foot to the refining laboratories. For secrecy and protection, they pay money all along the line of transport. The "fees" usually increase the further along the route the drug goes, and if officials must be bribed, their fees tend to match their authority. For police to track the drug on its way to international transport points means uncovering countless, ever-changing, inconspicuous routes of concealment.

The load of heroin or morphine base soon reaches a port or airfield from which it will leave the country. At this point, each kilogram may be worth $80,000 or more to the principal merchant who has bought it from the regional suppliers, and it represents millions of dollars to American buyers.

Sometimes private planes or boats carry the drugs on the final leg of the journey across the ocean to the United States. But most often, the heroin is smuggled out on commercial planes or ships. Unless customs officials are tipped off, their chances of intercepting the heroin are very slim. Police would have to tear apart every kind of commercial and personal cargo to find even a few small caches of the drug. Dogs trained to sniff out heroin sometimes help, but heroin is not strongly odorous, and it is usually carefully hidden away in commercial shipments of automobiles, TV sets, and other manufactured goods. In addition, many smuggling operations pay individuals thousands of dollars to carry heroin on their bodies. Frequently, even body searches are useless because the smugglers often swallow small elastic balloons stuffed with the heroin. After passing through customs, they either vomit or excrete the smuggled goods. Of course, if the balloon bursts too soon, the smuggler can die of an overdose.

The arrival of heroin in the United States, usually in New York City, requires very quick marketing and reaps still more profits. The importer cuts (dilutes) the pure drug with white powders such as quinine or with milk-sugar (lactose), which resemble heroin. The heroin, which is now only 50% pure, is resold to a distributor for as much as four times the purchase price. Distributors typically set up "factories" in inconspicuous apartments and hire people who work around the clock to cut the product's purity even more. In a day or two, the heroin will be packaged in foil or plastic "quarter bag" units of about 5% purity. A kilogram, or kilo, of pure

In the midst of the war between Iran and Iraq, a guerrilla fighter stationed on the border of the two countries shows his wife how to use a foreign-made G-3 rifle. Profits from large quantities of opium smuggled out of Iran may help to finance this war.

heroin can become 40,000 such bags, each of which can be sold on the street to addicts for about $50. Thus, as little as $500 of raw opium from the poppy field can yield $2 million of street heroin! And some addicts may need to consume several quarter bags each day to avoid withdrawal. The several tons of heroin that enter the United States annually yield billions of dollars in tax-free profits.

As in the nations that grow the opium, traffickers in the United States pay for secrecy and protection with illegal profits, and consequently often bring corruption to the communities where they operate. An innocent-looking child is sometimes hired at $50 to $100 a day to be a "mule," the person who delivers heroin to addicts, and so protects traffickers from arrest. If arrested, the child is not subject to adult felony charges. Traffickers fortify their warehouses with concrete and steel so that competitors will not steal their heroin and so that if the police raid them, there will be time to escape or remove the drugs. They hire lookouts with walkie-talkies to alert them to dangers in the neighborhood, they buy the guns they need to do their own policing, and they pay off authorities who are willing to be bribed. If need be, the top operators have money to buy the best legal defense available. However, it is characteristic of the drug business that the real bosses of the black market do not involve them-

A Thai woman and her daughter smash open dried opium poppies looking for seeds that will be used to plant next year's crop. The countries of Thailand, Burma, and Laos became the principal source of the world's heroin in the 1970s.

selves in the actual handling and distributing of the drugs —
they make the deals and the money and stay anonymous to
the street dealers, and even to most of the middlemen.

Heroin and Street Crime in the United States

The profits from the heroin trade are ultimately paid for by
heroin users and by the innocent people from whom addicts
steal in order to support their habits. In some poor cities of
southeast Asia, where an injection of heroin costs no more
than a glass of beer, the street crime caused by addicts is not
as devastating as it is in wealthier Western nations, where
heroin is far more costly. In the United States, robbery, burglary, and theft become a career for heroin addicts. Prosti-

*A drug-sniffing dog
rips open a package
containing illegal
substances. In spite
of growing federal
surveillance efforts,
most experts believe
that less than 10% of
the supply of refined
heroin intended for
the United States
is seized by
the authorities.*

UPI/BETTMANN NEWSPHOTOS

58

tution often becomes the principal livelihood for many female addicts and for some male addicts as well. On both the East and West Coasts, addicts commit an average of three to four felonies apiece every week — more if they are heavy users. Studies show more than one-fourth of all street crime in New York City is committed by heroin users seeking money for drugs. Studies show that more than 20% of all prison inmates are heroin addicts; inmates who are nonaddicted heroin users and users of other drugs have committed, on the average, less than half as many crimes as heroin addicts; and inmates who do not use any drugs have committed one-seventh as many crimes.

Such studies confirm that with their habits costing up to $100 a day or more, the hundreds of thousands of U.S. heroin addicts take an enormous toll on property and inflict

Heroin is extremely difficult to detect because it has no strong odor and it is usually concealed in commercial shipments of automobiles, television sets, and other manufactured goods.

immeasurable suffering on people. Since most addicts stay close to their source of heroin, the overwhelming proportion of their victims are the people and businesses in their own neighborhoods.

Heroin Plus: Addiction and Multidrug Use

When heroin supplies are plentiful and addicts have the cash, they are likely to use only heroin. But even in good times, many addicts use other drugs as well. Most addicts become moderate to heavy alcohol or marijuana users before they try opiates, and usually they continue to use those drugs even as their heroin use grows. They frequently also use depressant drugs, such as barbiturates, as well as sedatives and stimulants.

Since the late 1970s, cocaine has increasingly become the drug that addicts favor next to heroin. The effects of the two drugs are quite different, but, like heroin, cocaine produces a powerful euphoria, particularly if it is taken by injection. Dealers often supply both drugs, finding that addicts may switch from heroin to cocaine to help them through times when opiates are scarce. The combination of heroin and cocaine in one injection, popularly called a "speedball," is commonplace among addicts.

Although there are heroin addicts who start using cocaine as a substitute for scarce opiates, there are reportedly many cocaine users who try heroin for the first time because they hear that it is very effective at easing the severe physiological letdown that follows heavy cocaine use. For the more than 5 million regular cocaine users in the United States in 1986, this means that their chances of developing even more drug problems are greater still.

Future Trends

Although there are encouraging trends in some countries, heroin addiction does not appear to be significantly decreasing. On a worldwide basis, the signs are ominous.

An international treaty, *The Single Convention on Narcotic Drugs*, represents the commitment of most governments to coordinate their efforts to break up major smuggling operations and the organizations that run them. Through international cooperation, police and surveillance technologies are becoming more effective, destruction of crops is easier, and more subsidies are being made available to poppy farmers who switch to non-opium crops. United Nations commissions and groups such as the World Health Organization are focusing more of their resources on understanding the problems of addiction and finding ways to help.

Many countries offer school programs to educate children about the dangers of drug abuse. Anti-drug citizen action groups are proliferating throughout the United States. Some nations, particularly in Asia, sponsor government campaigns to warn citizens of the dangers of narcotics and the severe legal penalties for using them. Many governments under Islamic law, which strictly forbids drug use, are imposing severe penalties, including execution, upon those who are convicted of drug offenses. In the United States, another factor may contribute to reducing drug abuse: the percentage of the number of people under 25 is decreasing, a trend that is likely to continue until the end of the century. Most addicts begin using drugs early in life, and people over the age of 25 are statistically much less likely to start using drugs than those under 25.

Heroin addiction in the United States fell off after its peak in the mid 1970s. But use of the drug, which was relatively stable through the early 1980s, rose slightly in the

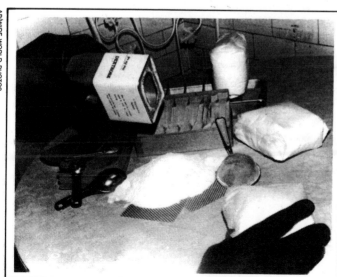

Pure heroin is cut with dextrose in a New York drug-processing factory. The substances that dealers use to cut heroin or cocaine may be anything from quinine to rat poison and can kill a user who injects what he believes is "good stuff."

middle of the decade. One reason is that the price of heroin has gone down, apparently because stockpiled Golden Crescent and Golden Triangle heroin has been put on the market and because heroin now competes with cocaine, which is very expensive. In addition, the use of heroin by middle-class youths and professional people is increasing.

At the same time, the pressure to reduce government spending may delay the upgrading of intelligence, surveillance, and enforcement work, without which there is little chance of reducing the supply of heroin. And no matter what penalties the laws in this country impose for drug offenses or how many arrests are made, without more courts and prison space the small-time dealers will not be discouraged by the threat of legal consequences. Not the least of the problems is continuing poverty and unemployment, especially in urban areas; wherever large numbers of people live in disillusionment and frustration, the merchants of heroin will find ways to do business.

In fact, social conditions are mainly responsible for the bleak prospects regarding addiction. In most countries, in-

Despite official denials, narcotics abuse is on the rise in the Soviet Union. The word on the fantasy-sized needle in this cartoon is "narcotics," and the drawing graphically illustrates the menace drug addiction poses to young people all over the world.

UPI/BETTMANN NEWSPHOTOS

cluding the United States — and especially in developing nations — the populations of cities are swelling at enormous rates. Refugees from the poorer countryside come looking for a better future, only to live in urban slums and shantytowns that breed the conditions of drug addiction. Even in Western Europe, increased immigration and rapidly changing social patterns are accompanied by rising rates of drug abuse, including heroin addiction. Moreover, social change can be a precursor to addiction, and instability and cultural shifts are at work throughout much of Asia and Africa. In contrast to the trend in the United States, in most developing countries the population is getting younger, not older. Just as it was "cool" to use drugs in this country in the 1960s and 1970s, many young people in other countries are imitating American styles, and developing American-style drug problems.

HELP US KEEP NARCOTICS OUT!

Thank You,

Myles J. Ambrose
U. S. Commissioner of Customs

THE KILLER

Reprinted with permission of King Features Syndicate.

Bureau of Customs ∗ Treasury Department

A poster warns against heroin, which is dangerous not only to individual users but communities as well — over one-fourth of all street crimes in New York City are committed by heroin addicts seeking drug money.

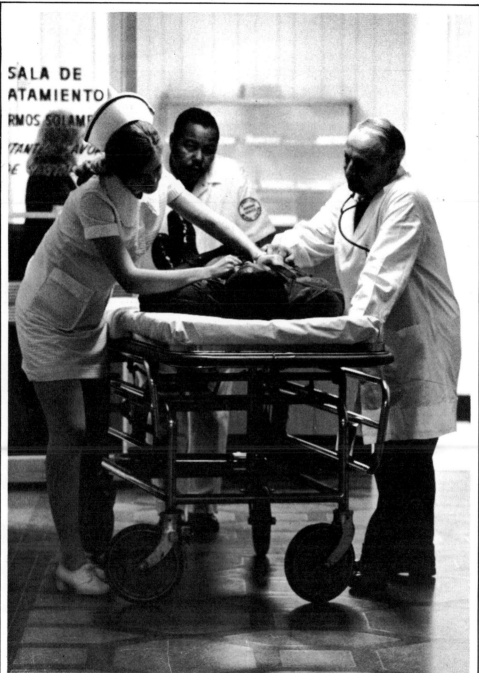

A single overdose of heroin can cause unconsciousness, coma, or even death. In some cases, the victim's life is saved but permanent brain damage results from a lack of oxygen.

CHAPTER 3

HOW HEROIN AFFECTS ITS USERS

*H*aving looked at what heroin does to whole populations, we now turn to investigating its impact on the individual — upon the body, mind, and personality. We will consider both the short-term, or acute, effects and the consequences of continued, or chronic use.

Short-term, Subjective Effects

All opiates behave similarly in the body. In fact, soon after heroin enters the bloodstream, it is converted into morphine by the liver and produces analgesia (pain reduction), just as all opiates do to some degree. But more important to many users is the experience of heroin's intense euphoria.

Heroin's *subjective* effects — the ones the user feels — are the most immediately powerful effects of any opiate. Injection into a vein brings the most intense and quickest reaction; it begins within seconds after the injection. For several minutes a pleasant surge, reportedly felt first within the abdomen, spreads throughout the body.

If the dose is heavy enough, however, this rush can bring on unconsciousness or even death. Otherwise, the intense feelings fade within a few minutes and are usually followed by several hours of gradually decreasing sensation, usually accompanied by sleep and lethargy. Feelings of dreaminess may be part of this sleepy period. But unlike opium, for example, heroin does not cause hallucinations or other distortions of the senses. Regular users often say that heroin makes them feel "peaceful," "painless," "protected," "warm," and "worry-free." But users frequently have difficulty maintaining their concentration and alertness while under the influence. Heroin also produces itching that causes many users to scratch their faces and upper torsos distractedly for hours after an injection.

Heroin can be distinctly unpleasant for many first-time users. Direct injection into a vein often causes the uninitiated to vomit, and other people find the effects disorienting and physically uncomfortable. Unfortunately, this does not always stop experimenters from trying the drug again, and running the risk of addiction. A characteristic of all opiates (and of many other substances, including alcohol) is that the user soon builds up a tolerance to the drug and must steadily increase the amount taken in order to get the same effect.

Acute Physiological Effects

The feelings of euphoria, warmth, and protection described above are accompanied by physiological reactions that can be observed and measured by doctors and scientists. Heroin is a depressant, which means that it reduces the key functions of the central nervous system. It slows the pulse and breathing rate, causes a drop in blood pressure, and relaxes the smooth tissues of certain automatically functioning muscles, such as those of the diaphragm and intestines. A person who is high on heroin may therefore exhibit poor coordination, slowed reflexes, and slurred speech. The pupils of the eyes are often constricted, the eyes look glazed or watery, and the face may have a feverish flush.

Precisely why heroin produces these and many other changes in the body is not fully known. But during the 1970s scientists and physicians made several important discoveries about the central mechanism underlying the effects of heroin. They found that, once in the bloodstream, opiate molecules attach themselves to certain sites, called *receptor sites*, on the long nerves, called *neurons*, that make up part of the brain and central nervous system. The euphoria and analgesia that heroin addicts so crave seem to be switched on when these connections between drug and nerve cell are made.

These findings raised further questions. Above all, scientists wanted to know why opiate molecules fit the neuron receptor sites like keys in a lock. Could it be that the opiates simply resembled other natural substances? The answer proved to be yes, and this discovery has profoundly changed and accelerated not only our understanding of heroin addiction but also much of our understanding about how the brain functions and how chemicals affect our moods and behavior.

Research teams in the United States and abroad began using mice, then rats, and eventually humans in their experiments, and found that the body produces a wide variety of extremely powerful substances that have come to be called *endorphins* (from Greek words meaning the "morphine inside" us). Responding to signals from the brain, these substances are produced in the pituitary gland and elsewhere, and are constantly released into the bloodstream so that they can attach themselves to the countless millions of receptor sites. Endorphins stimulate electrochemical messages that flow across the neurons and help regulate our responses to

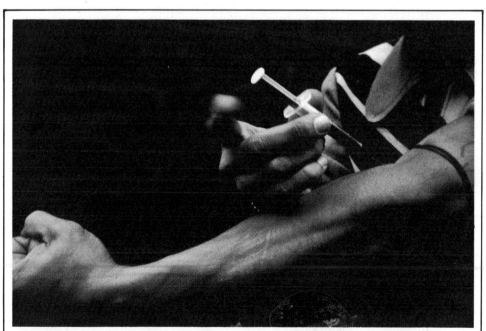

Heroin injection can cause serious infections: blood diseases such as hepatitis and collapsed or damaged veins are common among users, and acquired immune deficiency syndrome (AIDS) has become a serious threat to people who share needles.

stress, pain, and all kinds of internal and external events that affect our well-being. Scientists continue to study the very complicated changes involved in the body's lock-and-key mechanisms and continue to find new kinds of locks in the nervous system and new kinds of keys in the body's chemistry. It is now quite clear that heroin and other opiates mimic the effects of the endorphins. Usually, however, opiates enter the body in amounts much greater than the endorphin system was ever designed to receive, and the results are disastrous.

The Dangers of Heroin

Aside from the danger of becoming addicted, a primary risk of using heroin is that of overdosing, particularly if one injects the drug into a vein. Because opiates depress the central nervous system, reducing blood pressure, breathing, and muscular functions, a single dose of heroin can cause deep unconsciousness and death. Thousands of users in the United States die each year for this reason, and studies show that such deaths may be more common among people who take heroin only occasionally, or who are just beginning to experiment with it, than among heavy regular users who have become tolerant to strong doses. Even if quick medical attention saves the life of an overdose victim, the person can still suffer permanent brain damage from a lack of oxygen. Less profound unconsciousness under the influence of heroin can and often does result in serious injury if the user collapses suddenly or loses control of an automobile or some other kind of machinery.

Contrary to earlier beliefs, opiates (unlike alcohol and many other drugs) are no longer considered to be damaging, in and of themselves, to body tissues. But heroin users rarely consume pure heroin. The adulterants that dealers use to cut heroin or cocaine may be anything from quinine to rat poison and can kill naive users who unwittingly inject contaminated substances.

Injection itself also poses risks. Whether a person injects directly into a vein or just puts the needle under the skin, which is called "skin popping," improper techniques can cause serious infections, including septicemia (blood poisoning), which may result in the loss of a limb or even in death. After repeated injections in the same place, the veins can collapse or become permanently damaged. A user whose syringe is faulty or who out of carelessness injects some air into the vein may die in as little as a few seconds when a tiny bubble reaches the brain.

Even harder to avoid for many needle users are diseases that are transmitted by sharing the needles and syringes. Hepatitis, or inflammation of the liver, is one serious disease that has been common among needle sharers for decades. Similarly, poorly sterilized needles can carry the microorganisms that cause endocarditis, a life-threatening inflammation of the heart lining that is also particularly prevalent among heroin users. More recently, acquired immune deficiency syndrome, better known as AIDS, has become the most ominous risk of

Dr. Avram Goldstein (right) was able to isolate an opiate receptor in brain tissue, a discovery that may increase our knowledge of brain chemistry and lead to new ways of understanding and curing addiction.

needle sharing. AIDS is as yet incurable, and it appears to be invariably fatal. And as users contract the lethal virus and then, through sexual contact with others, transmit it to the nonaddict community, their drug habits bring death to the population at large.

The dangers of using heroin exist even for occasional or new users. But the dangers increase the more a person uses the drug.

Dependence and Addiction

The words *dependence* and *addiction* are commonly used today to describe a broad range of relationships between an individual and a substance or activity. For example, people described as "workaholics" are considered to be to some degree addicted to work. Similarly, many individuals say that they are addicted to chocolate. When referring to drug abuse, however, we assign each word a distinctly different meaning.

When opiates and several other classes of drugs (such as sedatives, depressants, and stimulants) are used regularly and heavily, they cause physiological changes to such an extent that the body will undergo predictable distress should use of the drug be abruptly stopped. This condition is called *dependence*.

As dependence increases, so does an individual's tolerance. It is important to understand that one becomes tolerant to both toxic and euphoric effects. This means that a heroin dose that barely gives a heavy user any pleasure could be fatal to someone who has less experience with the drug.

The suffering that a dependent person goes through upon abruptly ceasing drug use is called *withdrawal*. With opiates, the withdrawal syndrome resembles a case of the flu. Chills and gooseflesh, runny nose, aching limbs, abdominal cramps, vomiting, and diarrhea are all common symptoms. Though it can be very uncomfortable, withdrawal is not a life-threatening condition. But the drive to avoid "dope sickness" becomes a powerful force that sustains opiate use. And as every experienced heroin addict knows, a shot of heroin brings immediate, though temporary, relief when withdrawal is underway.

The withdrawal syndrome typically begins within 8 to 12 hours following a dependent person's last dose of heroin.

Usually the symptoms peak within a day or two and ease considerably within 3 to 5 days, but insomnia and irritability may persist for weeks. The severity of withdrawal varies with the amount, frequency, and duration of opiate use during the episode of dependence. More intense and sustained symptoms follow heavier, more chronic use. Psychological factors also play a significant role. Social support and one's physical environment during withdrawal, one's desire for abstinence, the availability of alternative opiates, and other factors affect the intensity of the withdrawal. A heroin-dependent person who is in jail and who still wants heroin may feel more sick than a dependent user who enters a caring and drug-free

UPI/BETTMANN NEWSPHOTOS

A 24-year-old heroin addict serves a prison term for burglary. The urgent need to get high has caused many opiate users to commit increasingly desperate acts of theft and violence.

environment with a strong motivation to get off the drug. Studies with opiate-dependent rats reveal that simply being in an environment where the animal has previously undergone repeated withdrawal episodes — a special cage, for instance — can cause withdrawal symptoms to occur again even when the animal is no longer dependent.

In any event, the withdrawal syndrome flares up and subsides relatively quickly, and normal physiological functioning usually returns in a few weeks or less. The person's tolerance to opiates will also drop off sharply. This means that if a person takes opiates soon after withdrawal, the effect

Many young children have contracted the incurable and deadly disease AIDS from transfusions of blood contaminated with the virus. Heroin addicts are especially vulnerable to this illness and are partly responsible for introducing AIDS into the blood supply.

from a given dose will be stronger than it was during dependence. Overdoses are especially common in such cases.

During a career of heroin use, a person may undergo repeated episodes of full or partial withdrawal. One method of withdrawal is to end all drug use abruptly ("going cold turkey") and suffer acute withdrawal. A second method is to be weaned from dependence with gradually decreasing doses of opiates so that the suffering is minimized. No matter how withdrawal is accomplished, a person is no longer dependent once he or she is opiate-free and has recovered from the effects of withdrawal.

Once dependence has ended, is a person cured? The withdrawal pains may have passed, but a more insidious drive — addiction — usually persists. As used here, *addiction* means the urge, or craving, to use opiates that can occur repeatedly long after actual physical dependence has ended. These urges are most often related to opiate use in the past. For example, a former user may suddenly want to get high upon seeing an old friend with whom he or she formerly used heroin. Holding large sums of cash, feeling very stressful and lonely, and, above all, having opiates easily available can also trigger strong cravings. Psychologists call this a conditioned response. Just as the dogs in the famous experiment by the Russian scientist Ivan Pavlov salivated for food, so addicts crave opiates when any of their psychological or environmental "bells" ring.

If physical dependence can be ended relatively simply, what about addiction? Addiction stems from unconscious conditioning, and addicts may truly not recognize that they are under the power of the drug and the things that trigger its use. "Don't worry," says the addict, "I know what I'm doing." In reality, with each new occasion of drug craving and drug taking, the compulsion becomes more deeply rooted. However, addiction can be greatly reduced and controlled by reversing the conditioning process. This requires abstinence, usually for a year or more, while the person adopts drug-free responses to drug craving. We will discuss this process in greater detail in a later chapter. But one vital point needs to be made here: even "recovered" addicts may still feel a desire for opiates. More significantly, if a person uses opiates, even after a long period of abstinence, the craving response can be strengthened quickly, and the individual will experience a rapid return of high tolerance if regular drug use resumes. So, in attempting even a limited use of opiates, recovering addicts court disaster. Dependence and addiction can return at an ever-accelerating rate.

The Impact of Chronic Heroin Use on Personality and Lifestyle

The details vary from case to case, but the downward course of a heroin addict's life is all too familiar and predictable. As drug procurement and use start to become more frequent, secretiveness is usually the first change in behavior that the user's family and friends notice. The user's time will be spent increasingly on drugs, either with other drug users or alone. Friends, family, and activities that were once important will be ignored. Disturbed sleeping habits may develop. Psychological stresses will grow as the user experiences and tries to rationalize and defend this new behavior. As tolerance to the drug builds, anger and depression may increasingly accompany the chronic user's high, even as the drug's euphoric

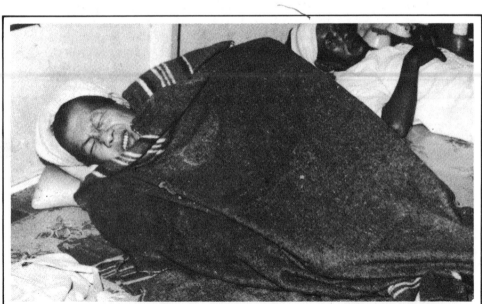

An opium addict in the first stages of withdrawal, one of the symptoms of which is dramatic chills — although the temperature is over 90°F, this man is huddled under blankets for extra warmth.

effects grow milder and briefer. Close friends and family often become the targets of hostility or are used as a source of money for drugs. Most addicts borrow heavily and use everyone they know to get cash.

Indeed, as addiction continues, those with whom the addict sustains relationships will usually become tools (consciously or unconsciously) of the addiction. Real intimacy between the user and anyone else will be all but impossible. For example, addicts' sexual relations are virtually nonexistent during episodes of heavy dependence. Chronic, heavy opiate use impairs sexual functioning and reduces interest in sex. The only exception is prostitution, which addicts often engage in to get drug money.

Although some heroin addicts can manage to keep their jobs, usually the urgent need to obtain drugs and get high rules out any kind of steady work or school schedule. Absenteeism, grossly impaired performance, or theft from the workplace cost most addicts their jobs, usually resulting in even more desperate behaviors: more drug use, more theft, more alienation and dishonesty.

Personal hygiene will suffer as the downward trend intensifies. Dietary needs will be ignored. Constipation can be chronic because opiates relax the smooth muscle tissue of the bowels. Medical treatments become for the addict merely a means of getting opiates. The long-term addict is usually reduced to a lifestyle that is entirely dominated by the drive to experience an opiate high. Flophouses become home, and going to "shooting galleries" (apartments or abandoned buildings where groups of addicts meet to inject their heroin) becomes the main social activity of most addicts. Theft and increasingly desperate acts of violence are the norm within this drug culture. In the end, the addict becomes little more than a tool and a vessel, obtaining and taking as much heroin and other opiates as possible.

In the meantime, the addict either prevents or distorts the day-to-day experiences that help develop maturity and stamina. This is why many former users, even after achieving abstinence and working hard to undo all the damage of their drug habit, find everyday life extremely difficult and suffer from deep self-contempt and hopelessness. Many long-term users express a desire to end it all with an overdose; perhaps many fatal injections are indeed deliberate.

Three Portraits

The following individuals are fictitious, but they are composites drawn from real life that accurately portray the lifestyles and personalities so common among the users of heroin.

James

Now in his late twenties, James had been an obedient and quiet child. He and several siblings grew up in a poor neighborhood and learned to avoid making trouble for their mother and to stay out of the way of their alcoholic, abusive father. Even before his teens, James turned to the streets for

The comedian John Belushi in a performance at Chicago's Second City Theater. After years of drug abuse and other self-destructive behavior, the actor died of an overdose of heroin and cocaine in 1982, cutting short a phenomenally successful career.

excitement. There, like his older brother and sisters, he could assert his independence and be seen as capable by his peers. His use of alcohol and marijuana increased quickly once he dropped out of junior high, and he began to commit petty crimes. By his 14th year, James was skin popping heroin regularly and soon began using it intravenously.

Since then, James has known a life mainly spent "chasing the bag." He has been in and out of the courts, prison, and, with hardly more enthusiasm, treatment programs. For James, treatment has been a chance to lower his tolerance in order

Studies show that a high number of heroin addicts and dealers come from poor urban areas, where increased immigration and a swelling population have been accompanied by rising rates of drug abuse.

to get an easier high, and going to jail is just a part of the lifestyle that he and many of his friends accept and share. Aside from his criminal abilities, James has developed few skills. Indeed, the straight life appears to him to be a more oppressive and pointless existence than the one he has. He would like to be a source of pride to the mother he loves so much and a good role model for the children he has fathered by various women, but he sees no way to achieve conventional success. He believes he will die from an overdose or from some violent consequence of his lifestyle, and he accepts drug addiction as his destiny.

Sue

Sue comes from a conservative middle-class family, and before she entered college — where, like many of her classmates, she started to smoke marijuana and drink — she never took drugs. She was eager to excel as an art student and had professional ambitions. To help her study when she was tired or had drunk too much, she sometimes used the amphetamine pills a doctor had prescribed for weight control. The pills made her feel creative and bright even when she drank. When she started dating a pharmacy student who had access to various opiates, Sue decided she liked their effects even more. She managed to graduate from college, but not before beginning to inject morphine supplied by her boyfriend and, when she could get it, heroin. After she graduated from college, she socialized primarily with other drug users and she usually had one boyfriend or another who could get heroin for her.

Sue has now been addicted to heroin and other strong opiates such as morphine and Dilaudid (a narcotic painkiller) for close to 20 years. She has experienced some periods of abstinence from these hard drugs, replacing them with alcohol or sedatives, but she has rarely been entirely drug-free for more than a few days at a time. She has had numerous medical problems, and from her many visits to doctors and emergency rooms she has learned to manipulate a network of medical professionals to get prescriptions for opiates. Her income has come mainly from unemployment checks, low-level jobs in art galleries, and prostitution when she is desperate. She also shoplifts regularly. Although she has been arrested several times, she has never been put in jail.

Sue still cannot easily acknowledge her addiction. She prefers to see herself as a professional whose career has been afflicted with bad luck, illness, and the failure of professional contacts and old friends to help out. But as she enters her forties, it is harder for her to deny how drugs have blighted her life. In recent years, she has made efforts to find legitimate work and stay drug-free, but then she gets depressed or ill and relapses. Usually the drugs available to her through her friends tempt her to go back to the drug habit. Most of the

"Shooting galleries" are often apartments or abandoned buildings where groups of addicts converge to prepare and inject their heroin, a ritual that becomes the dominant social activity for most addicts.

AP/WIDE WORLD PHOTOS

people she knew before her life was completely taken over by drug use no longer welcome her, and her immediate family has rejected her outright.

Mike

Mike was always somewhat mischievous but never got into serious trouble until his early twenties, when he and his girlfriend started taking the opiate Percodan which some friends gave out at parties. They both enjoyed the effects but she soon stopped taking the pills after she almost caused a fatal car accident while she was high. Mike continued using Percodan and felt that it actually helped him deal more confidently with clients at work. His girlfriend disapproved. He told her he had stopped, but secretly continued to buy the drug and use it more and more. Although Mike had heard that all opiates were addicting, he believed that as long as Percodan helped him and he didn't use heroin, he was in no danger. However, when he couldn't get the drug, he felt sick and frequently missed work. He eventually relaxed his scruples about heroin, and began using this street drug in addition to Percodan. His relationship with his girlfriend suffered, too, even though they both avoided the subject of drugs.

About six months after he started taking Percodan, Mike was caught stealing from petty cash at work and was fired. His parents took him in, believing that he had a "drinking problem," as Mike put it. They also gave him money to pay off his debts. But he was using drugs more than ever, selling his personal possessions (and even some of his girlfriend's) to buy heroin from his friends. Finally, a few days after Mike's mother discovered some jewelry missing, she found him unconscious in the bathroom with a syringe still in his arm. Mike spent a night in the hospital and then entered a residential treatment center.

He worked hard to restore himself to health and to understand what drugs had done to him. When he was discharged, his family and his girlfriend welcomed him back with love and support. His employer even rehired him. Soon, he and his girlfriend got married and everyone tried to forget the past.

Despite some strong cravings, Mike stayed drug-free for nearly a year. Then a dentist prescribed Percodan to ease the

pain for some dental work. Mike took more than the recommended dose because he felt it was inadequate. When he
ran out of medication, he called some old friends who supplied him with a lot more. On and off for a month, Mike
struggled against renewed urges to get high, occasionally
giving in and snorting some heroin. No one at work or at
home wanted to confront him about the changes in behavior
and mood that they observed. But it wasn't too long before
a full relapse was obvious to everyone; Mike had returned to
daily intravenous use of heroin and, increasingly, cocaine.
When new thefts were discovered at work, Mike's employer
had him arrested "for his own good." Mike re-entered treatment knowing he had a choice between treatment and jail.

*An officer inspects drug-manufacturing equipment after a raid. The several
tons of heroin that enter the United States every year yield billions of dollars
in profits for the bosses of the black market.*

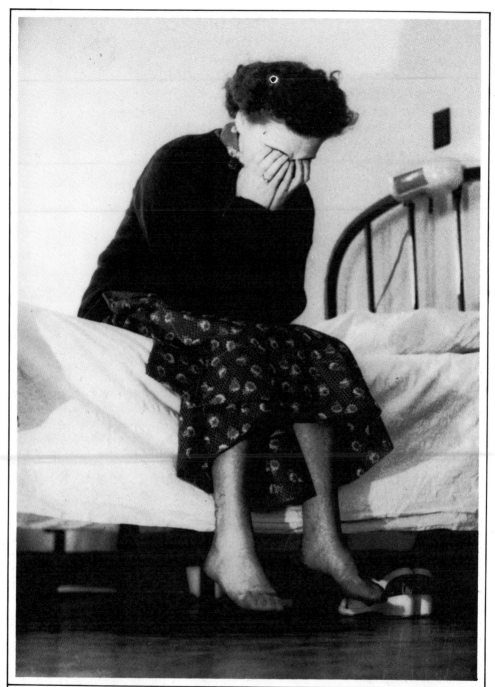

A narcotics addict struggles through withdrawal. Although for centuries drug addicts were regarded as victims of their own willful immorality, almost all contemporary authorities view drug dependency as a disease.

CHAPTER 4

THEORIES OF HEROIN ADDICTION

*F*or many years, heroin addiction has not only been the classic form of drug addiction in the mind of the public, but also the principal focus of professionals who study non-alcoholic drug addiction in general. Because it is a disorder that affects so many aspects of life, researchers in psychology, sociology, physiology, and various fields of medicine have investigated heroin's impact on human well-being. There is as yet no one theory of addiction that all the researchers agree on, but this chapter reviews some of the major ideas that are being explored. It also ties some of these ideas together so we can understand in a commonsense way how and why people become heroin addicts.

Is Heroin Addiction a Disease?

For centuries, drug addicts were commonly regarded as the victims of their own willful immorality. Even after it became known that chronic use of opiates produces physical dependence, people continued to believe that to develop dependence by overusing opiates and, worse, to use them again after detoxification indicated a flawed character and/or low intelligence.

Sharing the insights of Islamic physicians of a thousand years earlier, the British became the first to institutionalize another view. They felt that addiction was better understood as a kind of disease. And today, almost all authorities on addiction agree with this idea. But what does it mean to say that addiction is a disease? Does it mean that, like a cancer, addiction literally has a life of its own that can overpower even the most moral and responsible person? Or that something goes haywire in a person's brain and the only thing a person can do about it is take heroin? The answer is not that simple.

Disease usually means an abnormal condition in a living organism that can be recognized by a set of signs, or symptoms, that follow a standard course and that represent a threat to the well-being and full functioning of the organism. Heroin addiction does seem to fit this general description. The confusion and controversy over calling addiction a disease have to do primarily with how much conscious control a person has over beginning and ending drug use. Most diseases begin without our being aware of it. Invisible viruses or poisons in the environment may invade the body, or genes that were defective from birth may slowly begin to trigger serious prob-

Billie Holiday, one of America's best-loved jazz and blues singers in the 1930s and 1940s, also made headlines for repeated narcotics arrests. Her struggle with a heroin dependency brought national attention to the complex problem of drug addiction.

AP/WIDE WORLD PHOTOS

lems after years of inactivity. In contrast, drug addiction would seem to begin only if a person chooses to take an addicting drug. But if drug taking is, in a sense, self-inflicted, addiction itself is not; it develops not at the direction of one's will, but as the replacement of will. And, as we will discuss later, some people may suffer from problems that make them prone to drug use and addiction. However, for people who understand the danger of drugs and are careful to avoid the temptations, addiction is relatively preventable. Similarly, increased knowledge and responsible action make many diseases — such as heart disease, certain cancers, or tooth decay — more preventable. So the disease concept is also applicable to a definition of addiction; a person can rarely overcome addiction simply by choosing to be done with it, any more than a person can choose to get over heart disease.

But there is one aspect of drug addiction that distinguishes it from other diseases. Taking drugs, especially heroin, can be very pleasurable. So how can we say that heroin addicts have a disease when their problems seem to have so

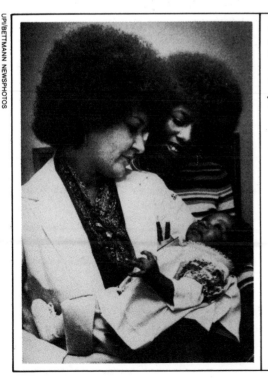

Babies born to narcotic-dependent mothers can experience withdrawal symptoms such as rigidity and tremors. Here, a doctor cradles an infant recovering from heroin withdrawal as the child's mother, a former addict, looks on.

much to do with experiencing euphoria? There is a possible explanation: one feature of heroin addiction is a drive for chemically induced physical satisfaction so strong that the addict's whole life becomes unmanageable.

It should be remembered that the disease concept is not a theory of addiction, but rather a way of thinking about the issue and forming questions that theorists then try to an-swer — questions about why people begin to abuse drugs such as heroin, how physical dependence develops, and why people who have "kicked" and "cleaned up" relapse so often, even though they know the dangers and have committed themselves to abstinence.

Conditioning

We know that opiates can be strong *reinforcers*, meaning that they reward the user's central nervous system with euphoric feelings and can dramatically relieve the distress of with-drawal. The more a person uses heroin and experiences these short-term rewards, the more *conditioned* the person is likely to become to the drug's effects. The reinforcement does not have to be powerful each time the person uses the drug. So even if addicts with high tolerance get a major reward only when they inject an especially large dose, that can be enough to keep the conditioning going strong.

Scientists often propose conditioning as the central dy-namic of heroin addiction. Experiments with laboratory an-imals such as rats and monkeys, which have nervous systems like ours, have proved conclusively the powerful reinforcing properties of morphine and heroin. But human responses are complicated by many other factors, such as personality and social environment. In addition, no one knows exactly why reinforcement operates in the nervous system of either ani-mals or humans. So, while conditioning probably plays an essential role in heroin addiction, we need to look elsewhere to see how it fits into the bigger picture.

Personality Factors

Whereas many people still characterize heroin addicts as im-moral, psychiatrists try to understand what lies behind their deviant attitudes and behaviors. For example, recent studies have demonstrated that heroin addicts have typically been more deviant in their youth than other people, but we cannot say why. In some of the earlier studies of addicts who were evaluated in prisons or while they were actively engaged in their addict lifestyles, heroin users frequently demonstrated the kinds of thinking and behaviors that psychiatrists call *sociopathic*. A sociopath is considered to be lacking the instincts that are essential for forming caring human relationships and to be resistant to the lessons of experience. Sociopaths are manipulative and devious, and they are always apt to blame others for the problems their own behaviors cause. The psychological concept of the addict as sociopath thus fits the old stereotype of the "bad" addict.

As a result, the psychiatrists who began modern testing and evaluation of addicts at the Addiction Research Center in Lexington, Kentucky, during the 1930s and 1940s expected to learn more about the criminal mind. But both the Lexington studies and extensive psychosocial research conducted since that time failed to define a particular personality profile that characterized most addicts or that suggested something about a common criminal tendency. Instead, the

"It is easier to get heroin than to get liquor," commented this teenage ex-addict from Queens, New York, who spoke to the Senate Government Operations subcommittee about his experience with drugs.

researchers encountered a great range of personality features. Most experts now think that the earlier findings were based on observation of the effects of addiction and addicted life-styles, and on the possibility that the more sociopathic addicts were the ones most likely to be imprisoned and written about. Difficulties in assessing the true personalities of heavy drug users continue because it is quite difficult to know whether an addict's thoughts, feelings, and behaviors are the result of the addiction experience or whether they preceded and con-tributed to the addiction.

Since the 1960s, new characterizations of the addict have begun to replace the sociopathic one. Various psychological needs have been cited by theorists as factors that drive some people to use drugs — and in particular to use heroin. Today, the term *addictive personality* is used to described a person with these overpowering needs. Like the disease concept, the addictive personality concept is only a way of thinking about the issue and not a theory or a set of facts. The term is probably used most consistently to refer to people who, for one reason or another, are thought to have an obsession with drugs, food, dependent relationships, or certain activities such as gambling or even shopping, and who can never really end their addiction but can only switch from one abnormal attachment to another.

Most authorities in the field of addiction think that a better way to understand why people become addicted is to consider the *proneness* (the vulnerability or tendency toward

Some psychological studies suggest that low self-esteem, which is one effect of alcoholism, is often present in potential heroin addicts as well.

ART RESOURCE

addiction) that a person might have. Following are a few of the major personality characteristics that are believed to make an individual prone to drug abuse.

Personality and Addiction

One psychological condition widely seen in heroin addicts is low self-esteem — which includes the belief that one is a failure or incompetent, related feelings of hopelessness, and sometimes general psychological depression. Some psychologists have said that heroin addicts suffer from a disorder named *hypophoria*, a kind of depression that is specifically related to low self-esteem. "Why shouldn't I take drugs if they make me feel good? I'm a loser anyway" is the presumed attitude of this kind of person.

Another common observation is that heroin addicts often seem to be strangely dependent on one family member or on the family as a whole for emotional support and acceptance, or develop an unusual attachment to a spouse or lover. Some theorists interpret this behavior as signaling problems with *individuation*, the maturation process of establishing one's own sense of identity and one's capacities for independent choice and actions. Since many addicts begin using drugs in adolescence, one possibility is that a very troubled individuation process made them prone to using drugs like heroin to get immediate feelings of warmth and security. Another possibility is that addiction in adolescence causes users to get stuck in immature stages of individuation.

Psychiatrists who have paid close attention to their addicted patients' unconscious psychological processes suggest that addicts suffer from repressed or buried feelings, such as grief or anger, that they feel are too powerful to let out. Sometimes the cause of the anger is thought to be the absence of sufficient parental love in childhood. Sometimes it is associated with the loss or death of a close family member or other important person. Increasingly, physical and sexual abuse are being considered as possible causes for repressed anger or sadness. Sociologists say that oppressive living conditions contribute to feelings of rage or abandonment that the addict finds too powerful to acknowledge consciously and cope with. Because heroin initially suppresses mental pain and angry feelings, its use is sometimes regarded by psychiatrists as a form of self-medication for unconscious emotional disturbances.

Still another theory about unconscious reasons for using drugs is put forth by therapists who observe families as social systems. They believe that the addict is often unconsciously acting out the whole family's psychological problems. This theory also points to the role of other family members who, also unconsciously, may even be getting satisfaction from the addiction. A relatively simple example of the family-system theory might be that of an abusive husband, his wife, and their addicted son. The son's addiction serves as an excuse for the parents to avoid their own problems, punishes the father, numbs the son to his anger, and gives the mother a person to whom she can devote special care and from whom she can get loving gratitude. The family-system theory says that, like the addict, all the other family members tend to get locked into positions and attitudes that keep the drug use going because that is easier than focusing on their real problems.

Several of the above theories can be put under the general heading of *adaptive* theories about heroin use. They assert that psychological conditions may make people prone to using heroin in order to adapt to difficult conditions that they do not have the strength to handle unaided but are not actually trying to escape from. Many addicts confirm that when they began to use heroin they found that it gave them the feelings of security and confidence they lacked; that the drug made them feel better able to handle inner conflict, personal relationships, and sexual intimacy; and that it generally made them feel "more together."

There is, however, a popular theory that suggests a very different reason for heroin use. The theory proposes that, because of their low self-esteem, some people become addicted in order to punish themselves or slowly commit suicide. After years of addiction, it is not uncommon for heroin addicts to support this theory. They may at times express a great deal of self-hatred and are quite willing to believe that their continued injection of heroin, near overdoses, and close brushes with death and disaster must relate to self-destructive desires. However, few addicts begin their drug careers conscious of any "death wish" or pursuit of pain, and therefore if these feelings are at work, they probably begin unconsciously and develop well into the addictive experience.

In contrast to either the adaptive or self-destruction explanations, another theory of addiction makes the case that because psychological and ego development have been impaired, some people have an abnormally low ability to delay gratification. Thus, a person may have strong needs for pleasure that cannot be met through the conventional means of applying oneself to a sustained task. Such a person may be prone to finding the very quick and intense effects of drugs — however spurious and destructive they may be in the long run — all too appealing.

A theme that runs through many theories about the addict's personality is that drug users are often responding to feelings of emptiness and futility. Unlike depression or low self-esteem, this psychological state is said to come not from the person's own problems but from a perception that there is nothing worth striving for and that life in general is meaningless. Psychologists sometimes call this the *existential factor* because it relates to basic questions about the purpose of existence. The pursuit of dangers and thrills that characterizes the lives of some drug users may be their way of getting in touch with their own life force, and drugs may add to the excitement. For others who suffer from existential emptiness, heroin may seem to numb the pain of feeling that life is pointless.

UPI/BETTMANN NEWSPHOTOS

A special assistant attorney general for drug abuse law enforcement displays a map detailing plans to disrupt heroin traffic in 1972. Although heroin addiction in the United States has declined since its peak in the early 1970s, statistics show that heroin use is on the rise again.

Many people — particularly members of organizations such as Alcoholics Anonymous (AA) and its companion organization Narcotics Anonymous (NA) — interpret any psychological suffering that leads to the use of heroin as an escape or an adaptive "crutch," to be a sign of spiritual impairment. Spirituality in this case refers to feeling connected with an ultimate and nourishing reality, whether it is God or some other source of meaning and strength. These spiritual doctrines about addiction state that if a person lacks faith and does not live as that faith prescribes, the pain and emptiness of life can make drugs dangerously seductive; moreover, if a person does become addicted, then only faith in a "higher power" (the term used by AA and NA) can free the person from that slavery.

Social Factors

No individual, not even the profoundly isolated heroin addict, lacks a social setting and a social history. Everything we feel and do occurs in the context of our relationships with other

Rates of heroin use are high in both rapidly changing traditional cultures and in modern urban neighborhoods. Some sociologists believe that weakened social controls are a significant cause of drug abuse.

THE BETTMANN ARCHIVE

people. The following ideas about social influences are among those that figure most prominently in theories of heroin addiction.

Availability

Making heroin available is surely the most obvious part that other people can play in the development of any individual's addiction; research shows that when drug supplies increase, the rate of new addictions usually does, too. But the availability of heroin alone is not enough to get a person started. Consider the historical cases of India and Turkey, where top-grade opium was grown in abundance for years. Those societies never had the addiction problems of the nations they supplied. And within a given society (the United States, for example), some population groups have had much higher addiction rates than others, even though opiates were widely available to all groups. If, instead of focusing on availability, we focus on addiction-prone personalities, we still must ask why there are so many drug problems in certain population groups. There is no evidence that proneness to opiate addiction has to do with factors such as racial or ethnic differences, the physical environment, or the food eaten in certain cultures.

Peer Pressure

Most researchers believe that next to availability, the key social factor that determines whether a person will use drugs is the influence of his or her peers. Indeed, drug availability and interactions with one's friends often go literally hand-in-hand; users usually get their first drugs from their friends. Most heroin users begin using drugs earlier than abusers of other hard drugs, although they rarely start with heroin. Cigarettes, alcohol, and marijuana (typically in that order) precede heroin, and social research demonstrates that adolescent peers who use these substances are almost always part of the young user's circle of friends.

Of course, not everyone follows the example of others, and often a young person will have several distinct peer groups with which to associate. Therefore social theorists, like most personality theorists, view peer influence as a contributor to a propensity for using drugs, not as a direct cause.

Social Learning

The apparent power of peer influence suggests to many social psychologists that addiction may have a social learning component. *Social learning* refers rather generally to how we acquire skills and attitudes and take on certain roles as a result of belonging to a social system where such behaviors are modeled in everyday life by our peers. It is said that through social learning, less experienced peers are not just offered heroin or encouraged to use it, but are actually *taught* to use it and appreciate it. And, through the example and approval of more experienced peer users, they learn the lifestyle of addiction.

Slightly older youths, whose tough, daring, and "cool" behavior allows them to dominate their peer group, are the stereotype of the role model who sets the standard of drug use. But a role model can be anyone a person imitates for any reason. Research reveals that heroin addicts and abusers of other drugs are more apt than nonusers to have family members who abuse alcohol or other drugs. Some psychologists suggest that this pattern results in social learning of drug abuse within families; other scientists claim that it is evidence of genetic factors that run in certain families, making them prone to addictions.

Social Controls

A community's *social controls* also have a major effect on drug use. This concept has as much to do with the average citizen's response to drug abuse as it does with the legal system. Social controls are said to be strong when, for example, families in a given neighborhood share similar rules for their children, and neighbors are watchful of other families' children and quick to report to the parents any violation of those rules. Traditional cultures, like India's, frequently have strong social controls that make it very difficult for someone to violate standards of behavior without being exposed and quickly reprimanded by other members of the society. Thus, it is argued, even though opium was grown in India and was for a while aggressively marketed there by the British, opiate use was kept within certain limits by local customs.

Communities and cultures in transition usually suffer a weakening of social controls. When new populations move in, when economic conditions change significantly, or when new products or technology begin to change daily life, community standards may become confused, the expression of community approval or disapproval may carry less weight, and more deviance from the old standards may appear. Sociologists point to the high rates of heroin use both in rapidly changing traditional cultures and in modern urban neighborhoods, where change is constant, as evidence that where social controls are weak, addiction tends to spread.

Of course, living amid rapid change can also be personally stressful; so is living where crime and poverty are widespread. Continual personal stress, whatever the cause, is one of the most widely accepted factors that make a person prone to drug abuse. And where frightening street crime, high unemployment, or generally unhealthy living conditions are features of everyday life, personality disorders of all sorts — including drug abuse — have a much higher than average incidence.

Setting

One of the most significant modern studies on heroin addiction focused on American servicemen in Vietnam, many of whom became addicted to smoking or injecting the heroin that was cheap and plentiful throughout Southeast Asia during the war. Military treatment programs had very little success in preventing relapses among those patients who returned to active duty in Vietnam. But only about 5% of the soldiers who became addicted there continued to be chronic heroin users once they returned to the United States. A leading interpretation of this remarkable finding is that aspects of a particular *setting* can go a long way in determining how a person in that setting relates to drugs. In the case of the American servicemen, the stress of the battle, the availability of heroin, the attitudes and behaviors of peers, and the lack of effective social controls upon American military personnel in a strange environment all made Vietnam a setting where a high proneness to heroin addiction existed. In the United States, however, these same men were in very different settings, with which addiction was incompatible.

Social theorists frequently use a modified *set and setting* argument to suggest that the laws that have made private use of opiates illegal have themselves contributed to the spread and viciousness of heroin addiction. They say that these laws may have forced users into subcultures where excessive and compulsive use, antisocial attitudes, and criminality become parts of the social learning experience and are not the effects of heroin itself. Our society's reliance on drugs — whether prescribed or sold over the counter — for easing every discomfort we experience may also indirectly endorse drug abuse. Drugs are vigorously promoted for "tension headaches" and "sleepless nights," and drug companies urge physicians to prescribe mood-altering drugs for their patients. In the 1960s and 1970s, illegal drug abuse was often supported by the popular expressions "If it feels good, do it" and "Do your own thing." Many people believe that these social messages made increased drug addiction inevitable.

Psychologists have also observed that as newer ideas replace older ones — whether in the individual or in society — almost anything that suggests the past may be disregarded. Thus, when American young people were disillusioned by certain aspects of their nation's politics and practices in the sixties and seventies, many of them also ignored old warnings about drugs. And when teenagers begin to define their own ideas about adulthood, they may also begin to challenge the prohibitions of their parents.

Physiological Factors

The study of personality types and social influence helps classify different forms of human behavior and relate them to each other. There are, of course, other fields of study that may yield even more fundamental facts about why people act as they do. Let us consider what neurochemistry is beginning to tell us about heroin addiction.

As described earlier, the opiates are remarkably similar to some of the body's own hormones, the group of chemicals called endorphins. The discovery of the opiate receptor sites in 1972 and of the endorphins in 1975 heralded a deeper understanding of the brain and the nervous system. Initially, scientists thought that *enkaphalin*, the first class of endorphins to be identified, was the only opiatelike substance in the body and that its sole job was to help block the trans-mission of pain when nearby cells were injured. During the next decade, receptor sites of different kinds of endorphins, including several varieties of enkaphalin, were identified. Now scientists are finding that other kinds of psychoactive (mood-altering) drugs — cocaine, Valium, and several classes of drugs prescribed by physicians to treat mental disorders — bind (attach themselves) to other kinds of receptor sites. Presumably these additional receptors exist for binding with natural non-opiatelike hormones yet to be discovered.

Even though the receptor/hormone system appears to be more complicated than was once thought, it is increasingly clear that our feelings and behaviors are somehow affected by a symphony of neurochemical messages and electrical impulses that flow along the billions of pathways of the brain. When we take drugs that affect our feelings by getting us high, we are disturbing the remarkable precision of this sym-phony with a tremendous overload of "false" messages.

Our society relies on a wide variety of medicines to cope with everything from tension headaches to insomnia. Many sociologists believe that this unthinking "pill popping" helps to promote the abuse of dangerous illegal drugs.

An important current theory states that when a person takes heroin or morphine, the receptor sites become overwhelmed by what seems to the brain to be excess endorphins. Thus, the pituitary gland, where most endorphins are manufactured, gets a special message to halt endorphin production. Normally, the brain, which constantly monitors the body's hormone levels and needs, stops and starts the production of hormones very quickly. It does this in order to maintain exactly the right levels of the very small amounts of the many substances that keep the whole organism in balance. But when a person repeatedly floods the endorphin receptor sites with opiates, the pituitary gland shuts down endorphin production for an abnormally long time and does not easily resume normal functioning. A vicious cycle begins as the opiate user becomes more and more dependent on *exogenous* (externally produced) substances to cope with stress and pain.

In the 1940s researchers recognized a condition called the *protracted abstinence syndrome*, which addicts often experienced for weeks and months after their withdrawal symptoms seemed to be over. The symptoms of protracted abstinence — long-term avoidance of drug use — include milder discomforts than withdrawal itself, abnormal hormone levels, and other signs of physiological imbalances. The syndrome may be a signal of the body's continued battle to switch on the normal functioning of the endorphin system.

There is also a theory that heroin addicts are born with faulty endorphin systems. Another theory claims that they somehow develop endorphin problems before using opiates. If either theory is true, heroin use may become an obsession because it tends to correct a bodily deficiency.

Modern science is also reviving some long-standing ideas about *addiction to pleasure*, the concept that heroin-induced euphoria establishes thresholds of pleasure that are so abnormally high that the heroin user loses interest in more everyday satisfactions. This concept gained new credibility with the discovery that there seem to be receptor sites that are particularly pleasure-related. There is evidence that one group of receptors in an area of the brain called the *nucleus accumbens* is the place where endorphins and opiates bind and produce the pleasure drive of addiction. The pleasure region seems to be sensitive to many substances (including cocaine and nicotine), and it may well be that instead of wanting love, sex, good food, or the satisfaction of a job well done — all of which may be expressed in subtle endorphin activity — the addict cares only for the pleasures created by the heroin.

Indeed, the brain appears to be "wired" in such a way that heroin takes the entire system literally by storm; and there is no denying the possibility that chronic heroin use changes how the brain processes feelings and experiences long after drug use ends. If that is the case, or if addicts are really suffering from a pre-existing deficiency, then maybe finding the right kind of endorphin or substitute that could restart normal endorphin production would "cure" addiction. Researchers working on drug addiction and many other kinds of mental illness are pursuing just this line of reasoning.

Does all this mean that psychosocial concepts of addiction are meaningless? Not at all. It appears that mental states and behavior contribute to neurochemical activity rather than merely responding to it. For example, studies suggest that endorphin levels go up in people who think they have received a painkiller but really have not. Other studies show that endorphin levels in the blood rise when people engage in certain activities that they have come to find satisfying, such as jogging and meditation. And it is quite likely that helping people change how they think about their lives, offering support and concern, and guiding them to new behaviors can affect their neurochemistry.

UPI/BETTMANN NEWSPHOTOS

During the 1960s, American teenagers began experimenting with drugs. Although heroin was not abused as extensively as drugs such as marijuana and LSD, that decade did see the introduction of this most dangerous drug into the mainstream of American life.

Full recovery demands that a former heroin addict find new ways to have fun and to deal with stress. Healthy recreations such as exercise help reduce the cravings that often hinder recovery.

CHAPTER 5

THE CHALLENGE OF RECOVERY

*T*here is no standard definition of recovery from addiction, which makes it difficult to determine how often recovery occurs. A full recovery should probably incorporate major changes in lifestyle as well as abstinence. But even in limiting the definition to abstinence, those who evaluate recovery face hard questions. For example, does an isolated occasion of heroin use, often called a "slip," constitute a relapse? When speaking of the length of abstinence, how does the degree of abstinence and any continuing use of other drugs affect the evaluation? One must also consider the reliability of reports of recovery. Who is doing the reporting? Treatment programs interested in promoting their success? Former addicts who might fear acknowledging a relapse? Furthermore, heroin addiction has spread rapidly among new populations, and many new treatment services are still being developed. Therefore, the rates of recovery may be constantly changing. And finally, people who recover completely can be the most difficult people to track or identify precisely because they have so successfully shed their former lifestyles and identities.

Despite these complications, the fact that heroin addicts can and do recover is no longer in doubt. For instance, more than half of the people who complete long-term residential programs have been determined by independent researchers to be drug-free and employed years after discharge. Virtually every treatment program that has operated for several years can point to "graduates" whose stable lifestyles are proof of real rehabilitation. If you go to any large meeting of Narcotics Anonymous, you will likely find many ex-addicts who have been fully abstinent for years. And the news and entertainment media often publicize the recoveries of well-known personalities who talk openly and in detail about their own success in overcoming heroin and other drug addictions. A heroin addict who truly wants to get off the drug and stay off the drug has strong grounds for optimism.

But in one vital sense, addiction is clearly for life. Once addicted to a given class of drugs, a person retains a special vulnerability to active readdiction should he or she ever use that drug again.

Recovery's Many Dimensions

The first step in any real recovery involves the addict's decision to change. Such motivation is usually the most significant hurdle in overcoming dependency. Withdrawal is a relatively brief but trying experience, and getting through it gives many addicts justifiable pride and more resolve to take further steps.

But because the urge to use drugs can overpower resolve, recovering addicts also need to look at how drugs have affected their lives. Earlier, we noted that clinicians and researchers have cited a wide range of personality disturbances as being characteristic of heroin addicts. For instance, their personal values need deep, sustained reconsideration. Distrust of other people — especially of authority figures with whom addicts have usually come into considerable conflict — and distrust of their own basic capacity to fit in as normal individuals underlie much of the struggle to stay off drugs. For many addicts, drug abuse began in adolescence, thwarting normal personality development. For them, when recovery begins, there is considerable catching up to do. Sharing experiences with counselors, close friends, and other recovering people can be vital in this painful but restorative stage of reviewing the past. Much of the first few weeks of abstinence should be spent on this review, because it brings a person in touch with the past, points out the need for change, and helps identify problems that could lead to relapse. This period also serves to help the addict resolve feelings of guilt and to recognize the responsibilities that need to be assumed in order to build meaningful relationships.

One of the next priorities is to end relationships with active users. Even casual association with such people is risky for the recovering addict, since the incidence of relapse associated with continued contact with drug users is extremely high. A recovering addict who lives in a neighborhood with many users will face special difficulties. As hard as it may be to end such relationships, some of which may go back years (even to childhood), it must be done.

A recovering addict therefore needs strong social support — a network of new friends who do not abuse drugs, who do not stigmatize the person as a drug addict, and who can play an active role in the person's new, drug-free lifestyle. Recovery support groups are among the best settings for making new friendships early on, and they help avoid the intense loneliness that often leads to drug craving. Moving beyond the addict and ex-addict community comes in time.

Unfortunately, sometimes family and friends of addicts prove to be a major stumbling block on the road to recovery. In such cases they are called *enablers*, because their unconscious attitudes and behaviors enable the addiction to continue. Covering up for an addict's irresponsible behavior, failing to confront problems, and protecting the drug user from the consequences of his or her actions are common

A young lawyer relaxes by performing a yoga exercise. Unfortunately, many people in the business world turn to drugs in a misguided attempt to deal with job-related stress.

enabling behaviors that can issue from unconscious family patterns. If another family member or loved one is an active drug abuser, all the more care must be taken to prevent an atmosphere where conflict and drug craving can develop within the family. For these reasons, it is desirable that close relatives learn about the needs of recovery and re-examine their own family dynamics through group or individual counseling.

Not surprisingly, relationships between spouses can be the most problematic. Coming to see the past clearly often brings both partners a great deal of pain, anger, and guilt. Many marriages do not survive addiction.

In addition, sexuality and sexual functioning are secret concerns of many recovering people. Opiate dependence usually impairs sexual functioning significantly, although for some addicts drugs seemed an indispensable sexual aid, at least for a while. Partners in committed relationships must share in the process of rebuilding intimacy, sometimes with the help of professional therapists.

Recovering addicts also face the challenge of finding work. Research shows that continued employment is closely related to continued abstinence; certainly the ability to stay gainfully employed is a logical sign of rehabilitation. But many ex-addicts find the authority structure, the stresses, and the routine of the workplace alienating. And though they may

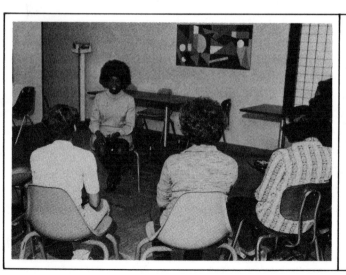

A group therapy session for recovering teenage addicts at a New York City rehabilitation center. This sort of counseling is particularly effective in helping young people to withstand temptation as they attempt to remain drug-free.

AP/WIDE WORLD PHOTOS

have a need for work that nourishes self-respect and continued growth, few jobs offer much of either. The past can plague the job search itself. How does an untrained person find a job? And how do former addicts with poor work records, whether or not they have marketable skills, account for their past to a prospective employer? These are some of recovery's most common and puzzling problems.

Rejoining conventional society also brings with it social pressures to indulge in some other kind of drug, whether it is alcohol or marijuana or cocaine. A recovering heroin addict must learn to say no. It's one thing for a recovering alcoholic who has abused no other drugs to learn that alcohol in any amount is dangerous; but it is often more difficult for a former street addict to learn the same lesson about alcohol, marijuana, and all the other drugs that always seemed mild compared to heroin. Former heroin users often see alcohol in particular as harmless — even as the very symbol of conventionality and a good way to ease anxieties in social settings. Turning down a drink may also invite unwelcome questions about the person's reasons for doing so.

And what are the dangers of using nonopiates? Research shows that new abuse patterns are quite high among those former addicts who use other drugs. By some estimates, more than 50% develop a dependence on other drugs, even if they do not return to opiates. Abuse of alternative drugs is only part of the risk; the door to an opiate relapse often opens with the use of alcohol or other drugs. Intoxication with any substance reduces one's control, and regular use can erode resolve and judgment, allowing old behaviors to creep back. Too frequently, the desire for opiates becomes overwhelming at some point.

Dealing with physical pain is yet another danger for the recovering addict. The nervous system does not distinguish between the effects of a legitimate prescription for an opiate such as codeine, Percodan, Demerol, or Dilaudid and the effects produced by an illegal dose. And laboratory studies have shown that even experienced addicts cannot easily distinguish heroin's effects from those of other strong opiates. Therefore, recovering addicts must always remember to (1) inform medical professionals about their recovery; (2) whenever possible, practice nonopiate pain therapies, such as meditation, massage, acupuncture, and nonopiate medications;

and (3) exercise great care when using medication, and have a supportive person monitor their drug use and reactions when pain medication is absolutely necessary.

De-addiction

Full recovery demands that a former heroin addict find new ways to have fun, relax, deal with stress, and experience satisfaction. Here is where many recoveries fail. Too often, not enough work goes into finding new forms of recreation. Most activities that bring pleasure and satisfaction require much more effort than drug use does; they demand more practice, energy, and social and skill development. So even when it comes to having fun and relaxing, recovery can mean a process of adjustment and effort.

Recreational activities that replace drug use contribute to the extremely vital process of recovery called *de-addiction*. This process is primarily psychological and involves the unlearning of past responses to cravings for drugs. Behavioral psychologists call such a process the "extinction" of a conditioned response.

There are established techniques for helping recovering addicts cope with this difficult process. For example, when a newly recovering addict first encounters an old friend who still uses heroin, or when tension or loneliness mounts, the person is encouraged to recall the problems that drugs have caused, become involved in other activities, and seek help from people who can provide encouragement. Many recovering addicts develop their own rituals to cope with craving drugs, such as telephoning supportive friends, reading inspirational literature, praying or meditating, and exercising. Pleasurable or stress-relieving replacement activities yield two important de-addiction benefits. First, as satisfying alternatives to drugs, they make it easier to say no to the urges to take drugs. Second, if performed regularly enough when craving develops, they can produce healthy, almost automatic responses to those things that trigger the drug craving.

Meaningful de-addiction requires real-life situations in which the former addict has an actual opportunity to use drugs. It is widely observed that drug craving decreases more quickly in controlled, drug-free environments such as hospitals or clinics, but the real test of self-control comes with reentry into everyday life.

For most recovering addicts, substantial de-addiction requires at least six months to a year of gradually increasing exposure to everyday settings and events. And although former addicts may always feel some craving, with care and commitment they can reach a point at which the craving is largely a thing of the past. However, de-addiction by no means makes it safe to resume opiate use. It must be stressed that use of any opiates will put the ex-addict at risk both psychologically and physically.

Personal Reawakening

One other event seems to figure in the personal accounts of so many recoveries that it bears consideration. At a certain point during their recovery, many people experience a shift in values and perspectives. Whether they see this shift as spiritual, religious, or psychological, few former addicts fail to acknowledge that recovery brings them to the deepest feelings of reaffirmation about life and its purpose. We don't know exactly how, when, and why this deep inner change occurs and how it helps support other processes of growth and development. Nor can we conclude that all recoveries demand a spiritual awakening. But we must recognize that a common price of heroin addiction is the collapse of one's core — the psyche, the soul, whatever one feels it to be — and that recovery often demands no less than the transformation of a person.

Feelings of intense loneliness often precipitate drug abuse in young people. A teenager attempting to kick a drug habit usually needs to establish a network of supportive, drug-free friends.

A teacher answers questions concerning drugs. A growing number of secondary schools throughout the United States have established programs to educate young people about the dangers of drug abuse.

CHAPTER 6

TREATMENT AND REHABILITATION

Our examination of heroin and heroin addiction concludes with a look at the principal forms of treatment used in the United States. This chapter starts by discussing some aspects of the legal system that provide an important background for rehabilitation and ends with suggestions about how concerned individuals can offer help to an addict or a recovering former addict.

The Law and Rehabilitation

Perhaps the most outstanding reduction of epidemic opiate addiction within large communities occurred in China after the 1949 communist takeover. The new government imposed very severe, quick sentences on drug traffickers, and addicts were subject to "rehabilitation" that involved especially hard labor and harsh political "re-education." The official punishment for relapse was execution. Many addicts who could, fled the country; many were executed. However brutal and inhuman, the policy was apparently effective. Although in recent years there have been unofficial reports of renewed opium and heroin addiction in China, most observers have agreed with official reports that claimed that addiction was virtually eliminated.

However successful the Chinese government's approach may have been in stamping out heroin trafficking and abuse in that country, such policies would of course be unthinkable in the United States. In dramatic contrast to the harsh methods of the Chinese, some people in this country propose a radically different public policy: namely, legalization of the private use of heroin. They argue that if heroin use could be monitored by medical prescription or legitimate authorities, the total social cost attributable to crime and the illegal drug trade would be greatly reduced. Tax money could even go toward the treatment and prevention of drug abuse. Moreover, some advocates of legalization believe that if crime could thus be eliminated society should allow an individual to use heroin — regardless of the personal consequences — as a personal right.

Advocates of this approach point to the practice in Great Britain that allows physicians to prescribe heroin for an identified population of addict patients. Nevertheless, heroin-related crimes and problems are still major social concerns in Britain. Among other things, many addicts prefer the high doses they can obtain through the illegal drug market, and the rate of heroin addiction has continued to climb as the black market continues to flourish. In addition, it is by no means clear that any form of legalization would prevent the diversion of prescribed heroin to the black market. Opponents of legalization say it would legitimize heroin use in the eyes of inexperienced drug takers. And given the euphoric

This Chinese poster from 1928 shows the forces of good health bludgeoning the demons of opium to death. Nowhere has the campaign against opium abuse been as intense as in China — at one time measures to stamp out drug abuse in this country included the execution of addicts.

effects that draw so many to heroin in the first place, it is not clear that a productive lifestyle could be maintained by most addicts. Indeed, steady employment is a problem for most of the British addict-patients. Legalization remains a controversial issue in this country.

In the meantime, the widespread abuse of heroin and related drugs continues to pose a worldwide threat to the social order. In the United States federal and state laws attack the problem from three different directions:

1. *Supply reduction.* The idea behind this approach is simple: the less uncontrolled heroin available, the better. Not only does less heroin reduce the incidence of new addictions, but it is known that when the supply is drastically reduced within a given community, more addicts in that community seek treatment. Thus, seizing large supplies of heroin is a major priority of the government. However, in spite of growing federal surveillance and the assistance of many opium producing and refining nations, most experts estimate that less than 10% of the supply of refined heroin intended for this country is seized by the authorities.

2. *Punishment of traffickers and users.* Stiff sentencing of convicted traffickers may reduce their number and surely expresses society's contempt for their trade. However, the resources of top-level operators make it unusually difficult to prosecute them successfully. And imprisoning addicts — who often also operate as small-time local dealers — has not in itself been shown to lower significantly the chances of relapse. Most resume using heroin as soon as they are released. Nor are there enough prisons to hold most of these people for even short sentences; convictions for possessing heroin without intent to sell or distribute usually result in some form of legal probation. But an addict's crimes against people or property may result in other charges, and imprisonment in such cases assumes a higher priority: to protect society, at least temporarily.

3. *Court-ordered treatment.* Because lawmakers have recognized that rehabilitation usually requires steady pressure and professional assistance, many laws allow judges to order addicts to get treatment instead of going to jail. Thus, probation and parole officers often play key roles in rehabilitation. And many treatment programs work closely with local courts to balance legal and treatment needs.

Treatment Programs

Drug rehabilitation embraces a wide range of professions, styles, and methods that reflect varied theories, skills, and experiences. The following pages describe the major kinds of treatment programs currently in operation in the United States.

Detoxification

Detoxification, commonly called "detox," aims to end physiological drug dependence. Once regarded as the essence of a successful treatment, detoxification is now generally considered only as the very important first stage of real recovery. Although one method of detoxification involves the abrupt and complete cessation of all drug taking, this method causes intense withdrawal symptoms and involves much misery and suffering for the addict. Therefore, detoxification programs usually make withdrawal much less uncomfortable and thus much less likely to fail because of intense drug craving. Such programs commonly administer to an opiate-dependent person gradually decreasing daily doses of methadone. Methadone, which is legal only by a physician's prescription, is a powerful synthetic opiate that, when taken orally, remains active in the system for more than 24 hours without producing the intense high of heroin. It therefore allows a dependent person to function reasonably well, with no drug craving, for more than a day after taking an appropriate dose. Most heroin dependencies can thus be ended with minimal discomfort over the course of a 10- to 21-day weaning period; during this time, the patient must discontinue use of all opiates except for the prescribed methadone. Recent research indicates that the hypertension drug Clonidine, which is not an opiate and which has few side effects, also reduces the discomfort of withdrawal from several kinds of drugs, including opiates. Other nonopiate drugs are also being developed and tested for use in easing withdrawal. Currently, however, methadone remains by far the drug most often used for this purpose.

Detoxification using methadone can be done without hospitalization, since opiate withdrawal is not life-threatening. But because the drug craving often intensifies as the methadone doses are lowered, addicts are more likely to complete withdrawal if they are in a controlled environment. Most detoxification programs try to ensure that extended treatment is begun as detoxification ends, but overall, it is estimated that fewer than 15% of the addicts who begin a detoxification program complete it and continue their recoveries. The success rate for real recovery is even lower for those who begin detoxification as outpatients. Most detoxification clients relapse quickly, and many enter a detoxification program only to reduce their tolerance and dependence, with no intention of remaining abstinent.

Methadone Maintenance

Methadone was developed in Germany during World War II as a substitute for morphine. It is a powerful dependence-producing analgesic (painkiller) whose effects are longer lasting but less intense than heroin's. In the 1960s, the American physicians Vincent Dole and Marie Nyswander and other researchers recommended the medically prescribed administration of methadone for long-term addicts, whose biochemistry, the doctors claimed, required indefinite opiate doses and who could not otherwise stay abstinent. This is called methadone maintenance.

AP/WIDE WORLD PHOTOS

A police official in Thailand burns heroin and morphine. This is done every year; in 1981, 702 pounds of these drugs were destroyed.

As of 1981, there were about 67,000 addicts on methadone maintenance in the United States. Almost all of them make daily visits to a clinic, where they take an oral dose of methadone. Clients who have demonstrated reliability are occasionally allowed "take home" doses so that they do not have to come to the clinic on weekends or during short vacations. Now, a long-acting form of methadone (L-alpha-acetyl methadol, or LAAM) that needs to be taken only three times a week is becoming more available.

Clients' urine samples are chemically tested on a regular basis to determine whether they are using illegal drugs, particularly opiates. However, moderate to high doses of methadone effectively block most opiate receptor sites from any additional opiates, so that even if a methadone client used heroin to experience a high, it would take a very strong dose to overcome the methadone block. Although oral methadone has a euphoric effect and may even, in stabilized doses, some-

The director of a New York City methadone center talks with a patient. Good communication between the addict and a trained counselor is essential to most drug-abuse treatment programs. Many agencies also coordinate psychological services with vocational and educational training.

what reduce reflexes and mental sharpness, methadone maintenance usually allows close to normal functioning as long as other drugs are not used simultaneously. However, methadone clients often abuse other drugs, particularly alcohol, which in combination with methadone can be especially potent and dangerous.

Daily maintenance doses, which were often 100 mg (milligrams; 1 mg equals about 0.0035 ounce) or more in the late 1960s and early 1970s, are now typically 30 mg to 50 mg. And many clinics increasingly emphasize their counseling services and support gradual detoxification — over the course of a year in some cases — rather than maintenance. The growing number of cases of successful, continued abstinence following methadone maintenance suggests the wisdom of this policy.

As a pharmacological control over another drug dependence, methadone maintenance is controversial. Some critics note that its use is most common in poor neighborhoods where rehabilitation of the community is really the major need. Others feel that methadone is "just another drug" that in the end provides no benefits either to society or to addicts who want to rehabilitate themselves. The original argument that for some addicts controlled dependence is the only option also remains in dispute. But surely, for many heroin addicts methadone has allowed stability and productive functioning. There are many sides to the controversy, and whether methadone maintenance lifts addicts up or holds them down will probably remain an issue of debate in the field of rehabilitation for years to come.

Opiate Antagonists

Another drug therapy for addiction uses *opiate antagonists.* This therapy works somewhat differently from other drugs and is intended to counteract their effects. Opiate antagonists chemically block the opiate receptor sites within the brain but are themselves not addicting or mood-altering. They have been available to physicians for years as short-acting preparations that were used to revive opiate overdose victims. Intravenous injections of these short-acting antagonists can revive even a comatose patient in minutes, as the drug binds itself molecularly to the receptor sites in place of the opiates.

Because opiate antagonists have a greater chemical affinity or binding power to receptors than opiates do, the longer-acting antagonists such as Naltrexone can serve a preventive purpose: protection against opiate cravings. If administered orally, Naltrexone binds itself to receptors for 24 to 26 hours. Therefore, recovering addicts can take Naltrexone and be rendered immune from the effects of any opiate for a day or more. The theory behind this method of treatment is that no matter what the intensity of their craving, addicts will be unlikely to use opiates since they would experience no effects from them.

Although known side effects are minimal, opiate antagonists have been used very little since their experimental introduction in the 1970s. Acting as a temporary chemical barrier to opiates, they do nothing to remedy the psychosocial problems of recovery. Like methadone maintenance, opium antagonists are a partial treatment at best. Their greatest value could be for recovering addicts such as medical professionals, whose work exposes them to opiates, or for other addicts who have a strong personal investment in staying opiate-free but do not trust their own impulses. However, moving from opiate antagonist therapy to "unblocked" abstinence remains for such people the greater challenge.

Psychotherapy and Counseling

At the heart of many forms of treatment is the communication between the addict and a trained counselor. The counselor may be a social worker, a psychologist, a psychiatrist, or an ex-addict paraprofessional. No one theory or school of thought on how to treat addiction holds preeminence in the field, and countless personal styles influence the way therapy is conducted. Individual therapy, group therapy, and, increasingly, family therapy are all used in the treatment of addicts. And many agencies coordinate these psychological services with vocational and educational training.

For many addicts, counseling serves first as a sensitive confrontation with the fact of their addiction. A good counselor — especially an ex-addict who can personally identify with the stresses of abstinence — can offer emotional support and a safe place for the expression of fears, pain, and anxiety. Group therapy is also good for this process because it allows addicts to share their common experiences and evaluate them more clearly. As the addict makes progress, peer groups can be invaluable in supporting continued change and growth.

Many psychotherapists explore the psychological roots of an individual's addiction and other conditions that may have contributed to the addict's difficulties. Marital and family counseling can help identify and modify the attitudes and behaviors among loved ones that may have contributed to the onset and perpetuation of addiction.

Continued counseling following inpatient treatment can help ease the recovering addict's adjustment to life without drugs. These outpatient counseling programs are the most common services for addicts in the United States. Because they may use any or all of the forms of therapy mentioned earlier and usually are open to addicts in any stage of recovery or addiction, as well as to users of any drug, it is extremely difficult to generalize about their value. What we do know is that the dropout rate from outpatient counseling programs is very high; and overall, the evidence of their effectiveness is inconclusive.

Methadone, a powerful synthetic opiate developed in Germany during World War II as a substitute for morphine, relieves withdrawal symptoms and allows these recovering addicts to lead stable, productive lives.

Therapeutic Communities

One of the most novel forms of drug rehabilitation treatment is the *therapeutic community* or *TC*. Therapeutic communities were originally proposed by psychiatrists in the late 1940s as special hospitals for psychiatric inpatients — the idea being that treatment could be enhanced if the social structure of the hospital environment itself stimulated greater self-awareness and responsibility among the patients. This kind of approach was independently adopted by the organization called Synanon, which began operation in 1958 in California as a residential community run by and for recovering heroin addicts. In part, Synanon was a rejection of psychiatric therapies, which the Synanon group saw as useless in treating addiction. Synanon relied instead upon the knowledge and insights of the addicts themselves. Typically run by former heroin users with strong personalities, other TCs were begun during the sixties and early seventies; they used Synanon as their model and greatly influenced the style and philosophy of the treatment of heroin addiction.

Synanon was originally designed as a permanent residence, in the belief that outside of a highly structured, drug-free, peer environment, former heroin addicts would quickly relapse. Today, hundreds of TCs provide residential therapy for thousands of clients, many of whom are chronic abusers

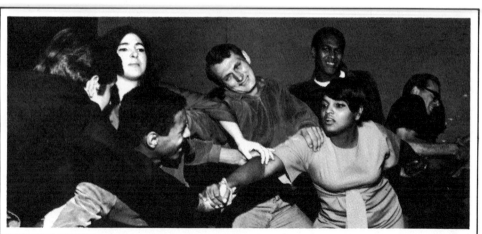

Profits from "The Concept," a 1968 play consisting of improvisations by ex-addicts, went to maintain Daytop Village, a rehabilitation center.

of nonopiate drugs as well as heroin. In most cases, TCs offer 6- to 24-month programs designed to prepare their clients both psychologically and behaviorally for life in the outside world.

TCs serve several important purposes. First, they are controlled settings in which new residents often undergo withdrawal from drugs quickly. Since most TCs endorse total abstinence from all mood-altering medications and refuse to indulge "junkie" behavior, methadone is rarely offered. In such a setting, stopping all drug use at once can be surprisingly tolerable and uncomplicated. Many clients also enter TCs directly upon completing withdrawal at separate inpatient services. Second, many courts allow addict-defendants residential treatment instead of imprisonment, in effect putting therapeutic pressure on them to complete the program. Third, the structure of confrontation among addict-residents appears to stimulate positive changes in attitudes and self-understanding. Most therapeutic communities also supplement their traditional self-help styles with professional counseling and therapy. The older, so-called *concept* TC philosophy involved tearing down the personality defenses of the addict with bitter verbal abuse and humiliating punishments and then rebuilding a new self-image, using rewards for more acceptable behaviors. Today, concept TCs usually incorporate newer psychological and developmental theories in their approach. Fourth, through vocational and educational training and because the upkeep and management of many TC facilities are performed by residents, they can teach new personal and social responsibilities as preparation for discharge from the program.

The dropout rate from TCs is high: 75% of the residents usually leave within the first six months. However, some follow-up studies have shown that as many as 90% of the clients who do complete treatment remain abstinent and employed for years afterward. Many graduates become TC staff members themselves, and so their employment is a kind of intense and prolonged aftercare.

TC treatment is not the answer for all heroin addicts, but clearly it has been good for many people who have needed a long-term, controlled, drug-free environment and who had to overcome a serious lack of skills as well as antisocial attitudes and beliefs.

Short-term Residential Treatment

When the vast majority of heroin addicts came from poor and disadvantaged populations, publicly funded rehabilitation programs dominated the treatment field. But as more well-to-do people have become addicted to heroin and other drugs, the number of alternative services has grown. Many private hospitals and health facilities now offer special services for both alcoholics and other drug-addicted patients who are able to pay for their services either directly or through medical insurance coverage. Typically these are 4- to 6-week programs that provide medically supervised detoxification, education about addiction, and therapy for both patients and their families. They do not provide the personality rehabilitation or the long-term behavior management and training of TCs, but they usually promote follow-up support (often through Alcoholics Anonymous or Narcotics Anonymous) so that patients can return quickly to job and family while still getting help in maintaining abstinence. Many of these programs are new and compete as profit-making institutions in the marketplace. They usually retain most of their patients for the full course of residential treatment and typically report that the majority of people who complete the program are still abstinent at 6- to 12-month checkups. Independent evaluations of their long-term success rates have yet to be made.

Self-help Fellowships

Alcoholics Anonymous (AA), which was founded in the United States in the 1930s, led the way for alcoholics to help themselves by helping fellow alcoholics. Narcotics Anonymous (NA) is a virtually identical program. It was formed by heroin addicts who were AA members, and its groups help people who are addicted to heroin or other drugs. These two organizations hold thousands of open meetings nationwide each week, where participants can talk about common experiences and difficulties. The fellowship among participants provides powerful support, inspiration, reminders of the past, and constructive role models.

The program philosophy of the "Twelve Steps" asserts that recovery begins with an acceptance that one is powerless over intoxicating drugs. It also says that the strength needed for abstinence and personal growth does not come from will-power but rather from a "higher power" — whether it is God or some other supreme being. For most people, the Twelve Steps thus make spiritual devotion central to recovery. As with many residents of therapeutic communities, the addict may undergo a conversion experience that profoundly alters his or her values and beliefs.

Though neither AA nor NA keeps formal records on participants and so can provide no data on their success, the growing voluntary membership of these two groups in this country and elsewhere suggests the important role that their meetings and philosophy can play in the recovery of the countless numbers of addicts. Many professional agencies view AA and NA programs as valuable adjuncts to, or even central components of, the work of rehabilitation.

How You Can Help

People in our society do not grow up to be drug-free without help, they do not acknowledge and confront their own drug problems without help, and they do not rebuild lives broken by addiction without help. Here is some guidance for offering your personal assistance to people with serious drug problems.

We can help most drug users by demonstrating that life can be lived well — even best — without drugs. This is not a moralistic cliché. Recovering addicts almost universally at-

ART RESOURCE

Unresolved feelings, sudden ambivalences, and resurgent drug craving can flood the recovering addict's psyche. Such difficulties demand that friends and family show understanding, patience, and a clear expectation that the person can and will take measured steps forward.

test to the value of knowing people who are good role models. Another basic need is for helpers to learn about addictive disorders and the process of recovery and, through understanding, to respect the committed efforts an addict makes to achieve recovery.

The best cure for heroin addiction, as for any illness, is prevention. Perhaps more typically than any other drug abusers, heroin addicts come to their "drug of choice" only after prolonged use of many other substances. Therefore, in helping to combat serious problems such as teenage abuse of alcohol, marijuana, or other drugs, we may be lowering the risks of future heroin addictions. And for every drug user who gets help early and avoids heroin addiction, a community is spared enormous suffering and cost.

To help an individual who is developing a drug problem it is important to see the danger signs, since the person will rarely admit to the problem without being confronted with it. In fact, many heroin users will admit to their use of other drugs or falsely claim a problem with other drugs (usually alcohol) rather than acknowledge that the real culprit is heroin. The visible signs of drug abuse are similar for many drugs. Typical ones are secretiveness, association with known drug users, disturbed sleeping habits, either a washed-out or flushed appearance, glazed or bloodshot eyes, slurred speech, unusual or unaccountable expenses, frequent mood changes,

PHOENIX HOUSE

Organizations such as Al-Anon or Nar-Anon can provide both support and guidance for the friends and relatives of drug addicts.

and deteriorating performance at work or school. The specific signs of opiate intoxication include abnormally constricted pupils, frequent scratching, and repeated dozing off. Even more telling of a growing addiction are thefts and missing valuables, withdrawal symptoms coupled with an urgent need to leave the house (actually to get heroin), puncture marks on the skin from injection of the drugs in the arm, and, of course, the presence of drugs and the equipment needed for using them.

What do you do when these signs appear? If the presumed user is only an acquaintance, share the facts with someone who is in a position to confront that friend or loved one with your concerns, as painful as that may be. Failing to do so could eventually bring even more pain. Initially, your words may meet with denial and bitterness. At first, most users deny to others that they are using drugs, and deny to themselves that they are in trouble. But by stating your observations plainly and without judging the person, you can show your concern and help to plant seeds of change.

If the problems continue, it's best to get additional help. Professional therapists can assist with sensitively arranged group confrontations that make clear the facts and concerns of friends, associates, and loved ones, and can apply concerted pressure toward change and, in particular, toward treatment. The more troubling the user's behavior is, the more treatment must be encouraged and demanded. Indeed, most addicts accept treatment only when the pressure to change becomes overwhelming and the support for drug use has all but collapsed. People who are close to the addict can receive support and guidance for themselves from professionals and from self-help groups such as Al-Anon or Nar-Anon. These organizations help people recognize and end their enabling behaviors so that the drug user can begin to experience more of the consequences of drug use. The family of a heroin addict should become familiar with the treatment resources available both to the addict and to themselves. Finding the right way to stop enabling continued drug use takes guidance, rock-hard determination, and love. It's important to remember that heroin addiction is a mortal threat and that treatment can save and restore a life. Seeking treatment must be seen as a step toward strength and wellness, not as an admission of failure.

Once the addict enters treatment, friends and family must support that treatment. Ideally, those who are closest to the addict should serve as partners in the recovery, learning about the therapeutic process, and (if asked by the program) participating in counseling sessions or other activities.

Partnership in recovery becomes even more important once the treatment is completed because the challenges of long-term recovery cannot be faced alone. No matter how committed a person is to abstinence, recovery means growth, and growth requires the guidance, encouragement, and accommodation of other people. And recovery is usually a bumpy road. Like immigrants in a new culture, former addicts are often insecure and hesitate to take steps that seem perfectly simple to the rest of us. Unresolved feelings and sudden uncertainties can overwhelm, confuse, and depress them. Renewed drug craving can be deeply unsettling. There may even be slips (back into drug use) that, if not confronted quickly, can lead to a full-blown relapse — a "fall" — that can destroy everything the ex-addict has built. Such difficulties demand that friends and family show both an understanding patience

A recovering heroin addict operates a pipe-fitting machine at a rehabilitation center in New York City. Vocational training can help build self-esteem in ex-addicts and give their lives direction.

AP/WIDE WORLD PHOTOS

and a clear expectation that the person can and will take measured steps forward. AA's famous motto says it well: "One day at a time." Long-term goals must be built slowly as a recovering person concentrates on the simple tasks of the here and now and deals with each need as it arises. With this in mind, families must stay informed and respectful of the person's plans and needs. Spouses and others must not be jealous of time spent with new friends at recovery group meetings. Old non-addict friends should encourage and welcome the person into new social activities that are non-threatening and non-stressful. And, of course, maintaining an alcohol- and drug-free environment is a priority.

Recovery from heroin addiction not only returns a person to normal life but frequently gives the ex-addict an extraordinary appreciation for the chance to love and contribute to others. To help someone recover often brings the helper a similar reward.

Recovery from heroin gives an ex-addict an extraordinary appreciation for the chance to love and contribute to others. To help someone else recover often brings the helper a similar reward.

APPENDIX

STATE AGENCIES FOR THE PREVENTION AND TREATMENT OF DRUG ABUSE

ALABAMA

Department of Mental Health
Division of Mental Illness and
  Substance Abuse Community
  Programs
200 Interstate Park Drive
P.O. Box 3710
Montgomery, AL 36193
(205) 271-9253

ALASKA

Department of Health and Social
  Services
Office of Alcoholism and Drug
  Abuse
Pouch H-05-F
Juneau, AK 99811
(907) 586-6201

ARIZONA

Department of Health Services
Division of Behavioral Health
  Services
Bureau of Community Services
Alcohol Abuse and Alcoholism
  Section
2500 East Van Buren
Phoenix, AZ 85008
(602) 255-1238

Department of Health Services
Division of Behavioral Health
  Services
Bureau of Community Services
Drug Abuse Section
2500 East Van Buren
Phoenix, AZ 85008
(602) 255-1240

ARKANSAS

Department of Human Services
Office on Alcohol and Drug Abuse
  Prevention
1515 West 7th Avenue
Suite 310
Little Rock, AR 72202
(501) 371-2603

CALIFORNIA

Department of Alcohol and Drug
  Abuse
111 Capitol Mall
Sacramento, CA 95814
(916) 445-1940

COLORADO

Department of Health
Alcohol and Drug Abuse Division
4210 East 11th Avenue
Denver, CO 80220
(303) 320-6137

CONNECTICUT

Alcohol and Drug Abuse
  Commission
999 Asylum Avenue
3rd Floor
Hartford, CT 06105
(203) 566-4145

DELAWARE

Division of Mental Health
Bureau of Alcoholism and Drug
  Abuse
1901 North Dupont Highway
Newcastle, DE 19720
(302) 421-6101

126

DISTRICT OF COLUMBIA
Department of Human Services
Office of Health Planning and
  Development
601 Indiana Avenue, NW
Suite 500
Washington, D.C. 20004
(202) 724-5641

FLORIDA
Department of Health and
  Rehabilitative Services
Alcoholic Rehabilitation Program
1317 Winewood Boulevard
Room 187A
Tallahassee, FL 32301
(904) 488-0396

Department of Health and
  Rehabilitative Services
Drug Abuse Program
1317 Winewood Boulevard
Building 6, Room 155
Tallahassee, FL 32301
(904) 488-0900

GEORGIA
Department of Human Resources
Division of Mental Health and
  Mental Retardation
Alcohol and Drug Section
618 Ponce De Leon Avenue, NE
Atlanta, GA 30365-2101
(404) 894-4785

HAWAII
Department of Health
Mental Health Division
Alcohol and Drug Abuse Branch
1250 Punch Bowl Street
P.O. Box 3378
Honolulu, HI 96801
(808) 548-4280

IDAHO
Department of Health and Welfare
Bureau of Preventive Medicine
Substance Abuse Section
450 West State
Boise, ID 83720
(208) 334-4368

ILLINOIS
Department of Mental Health and
  Developmental Disabilities
Division of Alcoholism
160 North La Salle Street
Room 1500
Chicago, IL 60601
(312) 793-2907

Illinois Dangerous Drugs
  Commission
300 North State Street
Suite 1500
Chicago, IL 60610
(312) 822-9860

INDIANA
Department of Mental Health
Division of Addiction Services
429 North Pennsylvania Street
Indianapolis, IN 46204
(317) 232-7816

IOWA
Department of Substance Abuse
505 5th Avenue
Insurance Exchange Building
Suite 202
Des Moines, IA 50319
(515) 281-3641

KANSAS
Department of Social Rehabilitation
Alcohol and Drug Abuse Services
2700 West 6th Street
Biddle Building
Topeka, KS 66606
(913) 296-3925

KENTUCKY
Cabinet for Human Resources
Department of Health Services
Substance Abuse Branch
275 East Main Street
Frankfort, KY 40601
(502) 564-2880

LOUISIANA
Department of Health and Human
  Resources
Office of Mental Health and
  Substance Abuse
655 North 5th Street
P.O. Box 4049
Baton Rouge, LA 70821
(504) 342-2565

MAINE
Department of Human Services
Office of Alcoholism and Drug
  Abuse Prevention
Bureau of Rehabilitation
32 Winthrop Street
Augusta, ME 04330
(207) 289-2781

MARYLAND
Alcoholism Control Administration
201 West Preston Street
Fourth Floor
Baltimore, MD 21201
(301) 383-2977

State Health Department
Drug Abuse Administration
201 West Preston Street
Baltimore, MD 21201
(301) 383-3312

MASSACHUSETTS
Department of Public Health
Division of Alcoholism
755 Boylston Street
Sixth Floor
Boston, MA 02116
(617) 727-1960

Department of Public Health
Division of Drug Rehabilitation
600 Washington Street
Boston, MA 02114
(617) 727-8617

MICHIGAN
Department of Public Health
Office of Substance Abuse Services
3500 North Logan Street
P.O. Box 30035
Lansing, MI 48909
(517) 373-8603

MINNESOTA
Department of Public Welfare
Chemical Dependency Program
  Division
Centennial Building
658 Cedar Street
4th Floor
Saint Paul, MN 55155
(612) 296-4614

MISSISSIPPI
Department of Mental Health
Division of Alcohol and Drug Abuse
1102 Robert E. Lee Building
Jackson, MS 39201
(601) 359-1297

MISSOURI
Department of Mental Health
Division of Alcoholism and Drug
  Abuse
2002 Missouri Boulevard
P.O. Box 687
Jefferson City, MO 65102
(314) 751-4942

MONTANA
Department of Institutions
Alcohol and Drug Abuse Division
1539 11th Avenue
Helena, MT 59620
(406) 449-2827

NEBRASKA
Department of Public Institutions
Division of Alcoholism and Drug Abuse
801 West Van Dorn Street
P.O. Box 94728
Lincoln, NB 68509
(402) 471-2851, Ext. 415

NEVADA
Department of Human Resources
Bureau of Alcohol and Drug Abuse
505 East King Street
Carson City, NV 89710
(702) 885-4790

NEW HAMPSHIRE
Department of Health and Welfare
Office of Alcohol and Drug Abuse
  Prevention
Hazen Drive
Health and Welfare Building
Concord, NH 03301
(603) 271-4627

NEW JERSEY
Department of Health
Division of Alcoholism
129 East Hanover Street CN 362
Trenton, NJ 08625
(609) 292-8949

Department of Health
Division of Narcotic and Drug Abuse
  Control
129 East Hanover Street CN 362
Trenton, NJ 08625
(609) 292-8949

NEW MEXICO
Health and Environment Department
Behavioral Services Division
Substance Abuse Bureau
725 Saint Michaels Drive
P.O. Box 968
Santa Fe, NM 87503
(505) 984-0020, Ext. 304

NEW YORK
Division of Alcoholism and Alcohol
  Abuse
194 Washington Avenue
Albany, NY 12210
(518) 474-5417

Division of Substance Abuse
  Services
Executive Park South
Box 8200
Albany, NY 12203
(518) 457-7629

NORTH CAROLINA
Department of Human Resources
Division of Mental Health, Mental
  Retardation and Substance Abuse
  Services
Alcohol and Drug Abuse Services
325 North Salisbury Street
Albemarle Building
Raleigh, NC 27611
(919) 733-4670

NORTH DAKOTA
Department of Human Services
Division of Alcoholism and Drug
  Abuse
State Capitol Building
Bismarck, ND 58505
(701) 224-2767

OHIO
Department of Health
Division of Alcoholism
246 North High Street
P.O. Box 118
Columbus, OH 43216
(614) 466-3543

Department of Mental Health
Bureau of Drug Abuse
65 South Front Street
Columbus, OH 43215
(614) 466-9023

OKLAHOMA
Department of Mental Health
Alcohol and Drug Programs
4545 North Lincoln Boulevard
Suite 100 East Terrace
P.O. Box 53277
Oklahoma City, OK 73152
(405) 521-0044

OREGON
Department of Human Resources
Mental Health Division
Office of Programs for Alcohol and
   Drug Problems
2575 Bittern Street, NE
Salem, OR 97310
(503) 378-2163

PENNSYLVANIA
Department of Health
Office of Drug and Alcohol
   Programs
Commonwealth and Forster Avenues
Health and Welfare Building
P.O. Box 90
Harrisburg, PA 17108
(717) 787-9857

RHODE ISLAND
Department of Mental Health,
   Mental Retardation and Hospitals
Division of Substance Abuse
Substance Abuse Administration
   Building
Cranston, RI 02920
(401) 464-2091

SOUTH CAROLINA
Commission on Alcohol and Drug
   Abuse
3700 Forest Drive
Columbia, SC 29204
(803) 758-2521

SOUTH DAKOTA
Department of Health
Division of Alcohol and Drug Abuse
523 East Capitol, Joe Foss Building
Pierre, SD 57501
(605) 773-4806

TENNESSEE
Department of Mental Health and
   Mental Retardation
Alcohol and Drug Abuse Services
505 Deaderick Street
James K. Polk Building, Fourth Floor
Nashville, TN 37219
(615) 741-1921

TEXAS
Commission on Alcoholism
809 Sam Houston State Office Building
Austin, TX 78701
(512) 475-2577

Department of Community Affairs
Drug Abuse Prevention Division
2015 South Interstate Highway 35
P.O. Box 13166
Austin, TX 78711
(512) 443-4100

UTAH
Department of Social Services
Division of Alcoholism and Drugs
150 West North Temple
Suite 350
P.O. Box 2500
Salt Lake City, UT 84110
(801) 533-6532

VERMONT
Agency of Human Services
Department of Social and
   Rehabilitation Services
Alcohol and Drug Abuse Division
103 South Main Street
Waterbury, VT 05676
(802) 241-2170

VIRGINIA
Department of Mental Health and
  Mental Retardation
Division of Substance Abuse
109 Governor Street
P.O. Box 1797
Richmond, VA 23214
(804) 786-5313

WASHINGTON
Department of Social and Health
  Service
Bureau of Alcohol and Substance
  Abuse
Office Building—44 W
Olympia, WA 98504
(206) 753-5866

WEST VIRGINIA
Department of Health
Office of Behavioral Health Services
Division on Alcoholism and Drug
  Abuse
1800 Washington Street East
Building 3 Room 451
Charleston, WV 25305
(304) 348-2276

WISCONSIN
Department of Health and Social
  Services
Division of Community Services
Bureau of Community Programs
Alcohol and Other Drug Abuse
  Program Office
1 West Wilson Street
P.O. Box 7851
Madison, WI 53707
(608) 266-2717

WYOMING
Alcohol and Drug Abuse Programs
Hathaway Building
Cheyenne, WY 82002
(307) 777-7115, Ext. 7118

GUAM
Mental Health & Substance Abuse
  Agency
P.O. Box 20999
Guam 96921

PUERTO RICO
Department of Addiction Control
  Services
Alcohol Abuse Programs
P.O. Box B-Y Rio Piedras Station
Rio Piedras, PR 00928
(809) 763-5014

Department of Addiction Control
  Services
Drug Abuse Programs
P.O. Box B-Y Rio Piedras Station
Rio Piedras, PR 00928
(809) 764-8140

VIRGIN ISLANDS
Division of Mental Health,
  Alcoholism & Drug Dependency
  Services
P.O. Box 7329
Saint Thomas, Virgin Islands 00801
(809) 774-7265

AMERICAN SAMOA
LBJ Tropical Medical Center
Department of Mental Health Clinic
Pago Pago, American Samoa 96799

TRUST TERRITORIES
Director of Health Services
Office of the High Commissioner
Saipan, Trust Territories 96950

Further Reading

Brecher, Edward M. and the Editors of *Consumer Reports.*
Licit and Illicit Drugs. Boston: Little, Brown and
Company, 1972.

Downs, Hunton. *Opium Stratagem.* New York: Bantam, 1973.

Hawkins, John A. and Grab, Gerald N., eds. *Opium Addicts
& Addiction.* Salem, New York: Ayer Company, 1981.

Jaffe, J.H. "Drug addiction and drug abuse." *The Pharmacological Basis of Therapeutics,* 5th ed., L.S. Goodman
and A. Gilman, eds. New York: Macmillan, 1975.

Stimson, G.V. *Heroin and Behavior.* New York: John Wiley,
1973.

Glossary

addiction a condition caused by repeated drug use, characterized by a compulsive urge to continue using the drug, a tendency to increase the dosage, and physiological and/or psychological dependence

addiction-to-pleasure a concept that claims that heroin-induced euphoria establishes thresholds of pleasure that are so abnormally high that the heroin user loses interest in more everyday satisfactions

adulterant an impure, inert, weaker, and/or cheaper substance, such as baking powder and quinine, that is added to a drug to dilute it, thereby often making it more dangerous to the user but more profitable to the drug dealer

alkaloid any of various basic and bitter organic compounds found in seed plants

amphetamine an addictive drug that stimulates the nervous system; it has been prescribed and abused as an appetite suppressant and antidepressant

analgesic a drug that produces an insensitivity to pain without loss of consciousness

barbiturate a drug that causes depression of the central nervous system; generally used to reduce anxiety or to induce euphoria

belladonna a nonaddicting, powerful, mood-altering tranquilizer obtained from the nightshade plant *Atropa belladonna*

codeine a sedative and pain-relieving agent found in opium and related to, but less potent than, morphine

de-addiction a vital process of recovery from drug use that involves the unlearning of past responses to cravings for drugs

denial continued self-deception by a chronic drug user about growing abuse and dependence

depressant any drug that decreases a bodily function and/ or nerve activity

detoxification the process by which an addicted individual is gradually withdrawn from the abused drug, usually under medical supervision and sometimes in conjunction with the administration of other drugs

dysphoria   an exaggerated feeling of depression related to low self-esteem

endocarditis   a life-threatening inflammation of the lining of the heart

endorphin   substances produced mainly by the pituitary gland that, in a manner similar to opiates, become attached to receptor sites on neurons, thereby helping to regulate responses to stress, pain, and many other internal and external events that affect an individual's well-being

enkaphalin   a type of endorphin that helps block the transmission of pain

euphoria   a mental high characterized by a sense of well-being

extinction   the gradual loss of a conditioned reflex

hallucination   a sensory impression that has no basis in external stimulation

hashish   an extract prepared from the flowers, stalks, leaves, and resin of the hemp, or marijuana, plant, which is smoked for its euphoric effects

hepatitis   inflammation of the liver

heroin   a semisynthetic opiate produced by a chemical modification of morphine and abused for its analgesic and euphoric effects

hypertension   abnormally high blood pressure

individuation   the maturation process of establishing one's own sense of identity and capacities for independent choice and actions

methadone   a synthetic opiate that produces effects similar to morphine and is used to treat pain associated with terminal cancer and in the treatment of heroin addiction

morphine   the principal psychoactive ingredient of opium that produces sleep or a state of stupor, and is used as the standard against which all morphine-like drugs are compared

neuron   a cell specialized to conduct electrochemical signals

nucleus accumbens   a region of receptors in the brain where endorphins and opiates bind and produce the pleasure drive of addiction

opiate   a compound from the milky juice of the poppy plant *Papaver somniferum*, including opium, morphine, codeine, and their derivatives, such as heroin

opiate antagonist   a drug which, when administered, prevents an opiate from having any effect

overdose   when more of a drug is taken than the amount necessary to obtain a desired effect, usually resulting in adverse effects or even death

physical dependence   an adaptation of the body to the presence of a drug such that its absence produces withdrawal symptoms

protracted-abstinence syndrome   a group of symptoms that persists after withdrawal symptoms have disappeared, includes abnormal hormone levels, discomforts milder than withdrawal itself, and other signs of physiological imbalances

psychoactive   changing mood, behavior, and/or thought processes

psychological dependence   a condition in which the drug user craves a drug to maintain a sense of well-being and feels discomfort when deprived of it

receptor site   a specialized center located on a neuron that, when bound by a sufficient number of molecules, such as endorphin or opiate molecules, produces an electrical charge

sedative   a drug that produces calmness, relaxation, and, at high doses, sleep; includes barbiturates

septicemia   blood poisoning, or the presence of disease-causing bacteria in the blood

sociopathic   a term used to describe a person who lacks the instincts that are essential for forming caring human relationships and who is resistant to the lessons of experience

tincture   an alcoholic extract of vegetable or animal substances

tolerance   a decrease of susceptibility to the effects of a drug due to its continued administration, resulting in the user's need to increase the drug dosage to achieve the effects experienced previously

tranquilizer   a drug that has calming, relaxing effects

withdrawal   the physiological and psychological effects of discontinued usage of a drug

Index

abstinence, 35, 42, 73, 98, 101–102, 119–120
  see also heroin, addiction
acquired immune deficiency syndrome
  see AIDS
adaptive theories, 90–91
  see also heroin, addiction
Addiction Research Center, 42–43, 87
  see also heroin, addiction
addictive personality, 88, 102
AIDS (acquired immune deficiency
    syndrome), 69–70
  see also heroin, risks
Al-Anon, 123
  see also Alcoholics Anonymous
alcohol, 23, 27, 32, 39, 60, 66, 68, 77, 93–94, 105, 115, 120, 122
alcoholics *see* alcohol; Alcoholics
    Anonymous
Alcoholics Anonymous, 92, 120–121, 125
alcoholism, 49
  see also alcohol; Alcoholics
    Anonymous
alkaloid, 24
  see also opiates
amphetamines, 45, 78
analgesic, 113
  see also morphine, medical uses;
    opium, medical uses
Anslinger, Harry, 44
  see also Bureau of Narcotics; heroin,
    efforts to control
aspirin, 19, 33
Atropa belladonna, 35
  see also heroin, addiction
barbiturates, 45, 60
Baudelaire, Charles, 25
  see also laudanum; opium
Bayer Company, 19, 33–34
  see also heroin, synthesis
belladonna, 35
black market, 39, 42, 54–58, 110–111
  see also heroin, crime and; heroin,
    distribution and marketing
bootlegging, 39
  see also alcohol
British East India Company, 22, 27

Browning, Elizabeth Barrett, 25
Bureau of Narcotics, 38, 42, 44
  see also heroin, crime and; heroin,
    efforts to control
Byron, Lord (George Gordon), 25
cigarettes, 93
clonidine, 112
  see also heroin, addiction
cocaine, 29, 32, 36, 39, 45, 60, 68, 97, 99, 105
codeine, 49, 105
  see also opiates
Coleridge, Samuel, 25
concept TC, 119
  see also heroin, addiction;
    therapeutic communities
conditioned response, 73, 106
conditioning, 86
Confessions of an English Opium-Eater
    (De Quincey), 24–25
counseling, 116–120
  see also heroin, addiction
De Quincey, Thomas, 24–25
de-addiction, 106–107
  see also heroin, addiction
Demerol (meperidine), 105
  see also opiates
dependence, 70
  see also heroin, addiction; heroin,
    dependence; opium, dependence
detoxification, 35, 37, 40, 42, 112–113, 115
  see also heroin, addiction; opiates,
    addiction
diacetylmorphine, 33
  see also heroin
diazepam *see* Valium
Dilaudid (hydromorphone), 78, 105
disease, 84–85
  see also heroin, addiction; opiates,
    addiction
Dole, Vincent, 113
  see also heroin, addiction;
    maintenance therapy; methadone
"dope fiends," 27, 39, 42
  see also heroin, public attitudes;
    opiates, addiction

toxic effects, 21
  see also heroin; morphine; opiates
opium poppy *(Papaver somniferum)*
  geography, 20
  products, 19–20
  religious uses, 20
  see also heroin; morphine; opiates; opium
Opium Wars, 25–27
outpatient counseling programs, 117
oxycodone *see* Percodan
Papaver somniferum see opium poppy
Paracelsus, 22
  see also opium, history
patent medicines, 31–32
  see also opium, history; opium, medical uses
Pavlov, Ivan, 73
Percodan (oxycodone), 80, 105
  see also opiates
Poe, Edgar Allan, 25
poppy *see* opium poppy
Prohibition, 39
proneness, 88
  see also heroin, addiction
protracted abstinence syndrome, 98
  see also abstinence
psychotherapy, 116–117
Pure Food and Drug Act of 1906, 36
purge therapy, 35
  see also heroin, addiction
"quarter bag," 56
  see also heroin, distribution and marketing
quinine, 56, 68
  see also heroin, distribution and marketing
receptor sites, 66–67, 97, 114–116
reinforcers, 86
  see also heroin, addiction
self-help fellowships, 120–121
  see also heroin, addiction

septicemia, 68
  see also heroin, risks
Sertuerner, Frederick, 24
  see also morphine
"shooting galleries," 75
Single Convention on Narcotic Drugs, The, 60
"skin popping," 68, 77
social learning, 94
  see also heroin, addiction
sociopath, 87–88
  see also heroin, addiction
"speedball," 60
  see also cocaine; heroin, use of other drugs with
Swinburne, Algernon, 25
Synanon, 118
  see also heroin, addiction; therapeutic community
TC *see* therapeutic community
thebacium, 20
  see also opium poppy
therapeutic community (TC), 118–121
  history, 118
tolerance, 24, 70, 72
  see also heroin, addiction
tongs, Chinese, 36, 39
  see also black market; opium, history
Treaty of Nanking, 27
  see also opium, history
"Twelve Steps," 120–121
  see also Alcoholics Anonymous
"unblocked" abstinence, 116
  see also abstinence
Valium (diazepam), 97
withdrawal, 35, 70–73, 102, 119, 123
  see also heroin, withdrawal
Wright, C. R., 33
  see also heroin, synthesis
Wright, Hamilton, 36
  see also opiates, efforts to control

Fred Zackon, M.Ed., received his degree in the Human and Social Service Program of Antioch College. He has worked with drug addicts in various clinical and research settings. Currently he is specializing in social and developmental factors involved in the recovery from chronic life disorders, and he is working to improve the effectiveness of self-help groups.

Solomon H. Snyder, M.D., is Distinguished Service Professor of Neuroscience, Pharmacology and Psychiatry at The Johns Hopkins University School of Medicine. He has served as president of the Society for Neuroscience and in 1978 received the Albert Lasker Award in Medical Research. He has authored *Uses of Marijuana, Madness and the Brain, The Troubled Mind, Biological Aspects of Mental Disorder,* and edited *Perspective in Neuropharmacology: A Tribute to Julius Axelrod.* Professor Snyder was a research associate with Dr. Axelrod at the National Institutes of Health.

Barry L. Jacobs, Ph.D., is currently a professor in the program of neuroscience at Princeton University. Professor Jacobs is author of *Serotonin Neurotransmission and Behavior* and *Hallucinogens: Neurochemical, Behavioral and Clinical Perspectives.* He has written many journal articles in the field of neuroscience and contributed numerous chapters to books on behavior and brain science. He has been a member of several panels of the National Institute of Mental Health.

Jerome H. Jaffe, M.D., formerly professor of psychiatry at the College of Physicians and Surgeons, Columbia University, has been named recently Director of the Addiction Research Center of the National Institute on Drug Abuse. Dr. Jaffe is also a psychopharmacologist and has conducted research on a wide range of addictive drugs and developed treatment programs for addicts. He has acted as Special Consultant to the President on Narcotics and Dangerous Drugs and was the first director of the White House Special Action Office for Drug Abuse Prevention.